Amazing States

Written by
Margaret Burda

Illustrated by David Sodac

Cover by Vanessa Filkins

Copyright © Good Apple, Inc., 1984

ISBN No. 0-86653-205-6

Printing No. 987

GOOD APPLE, INC.
BOX 299
CARTHAGE, IL 62321-0299

To the Teacher

This book was designed to provide extra reinforcement for the study of the United States. The word searches are exciting and fun for the students. They are easy to check and provide a springboard for further research of each state. They've been classroom tested and found very effective.

The teaching suggestion pages include a wide variety of activities: mobiles, collages, puppets, skits, time lines, short biographies, brochures, salt and flour maps, reports, and even simple jewelry making. The activities are tailored to emphasize the states' uniqueness. They are designed to cover the multiple components found in social studies.

The words enclosed in parentheses in the word searches are not included. An example of this is (Betsy) Ross. (Betsy) is not in the puzzle. Red Eagle (2) means that Red and Eagle are not written as one entry.

Some puzzles have a word which appears twice. If the wrong word is circled, then the state nickname will not be revealed.

Extra sources for some of the needed information should include: a U.S. road atlas, a world atlas, and a U.S. atlas. Other helpful sources are *The Dictionary of American Biography* or *The Dictionary of National Biography*.

It is my sincere hope that you and your students will enjoy this book as much as my students and I have enjoyed working on it.

Margaret Burda

ALABAMA

Cities
Birmingham
Elba
Enterprise
Huntsville
Opp
Tuscaloosa
Mobile
Montgomery

Rivers
Alabama
Chattahoochee
Coosa
Tennessee
Tombigbee

Indians
Cherokee
Chickasaw
Choctaw
Cliff Dwellers (2)
Creek

Famous People
Carver
Davis
Keller
Lee
Red Eagle (2)
Washington

Minerals
Clay
Coal
Iron Ore (2)
Marble
Mica
Oil
Limestone
Sand

Products
Chemicals
Cotton
Beef
Hog
Eggs
Oysters
Paper
Nuts
Shrimp

M	O	B	I	L	E	L	B	A	C	L	
O	A	H	E	K	K	E	L	O	O	I	
N	S	R	A	E	E	A	A	Y	T	M	
T	O	G	E	W	B	L	S	R	T	E	T
G	O	R	G	A	A	T	L	R	O	S	O
O	C	M	M	E	E	T	E	N	T	E	
M	P	A	B	R	C	D	C	O	R	O	E

P	E	F	P	S	I	E	H	T	O	A	N	H	M
I	R	E	I	D	L	G	G	E	S	H	E	C	I
N	Y	V	S	B	W	N	B	O	M	L	C	O	C
E	A	S	R	S	I	A	O	E	L	I	I	O	A
D	E	A	R	H	E	L	S	I	E	M	C	H	I	D
E	M	K	S	E	A	N	V	A	A	F	C	A	L	N
S	A	A	O	C	L	S	N	H	K	A	C	T	L	A
I	W	G	S	R	T	L	G	E	R	C	L	T	E	S
R	S	U	L	N	E	N	E	V	T	L	I	A	M
P	T	S	U	E	I	H	E	W	I	A	F	H	A
R	U	H	I	M	X	R	C	O	D	Y	F	C	C
E	N	R	R	E	M	M	A	H	W	O	L	L	E	Y
T	O	I	E

N	B	M	P	H
E	I	P	A	O
	E	P	G

State Symbols
Bird: Yellowhammer
Flower: Camellia
Tree: (Southern) Pine

Put the unused letters on the blanks below.
If you are right, the state nickname will show.

_ _ _ _ _ _ _ _ _ _ _ _ _ _ _ _ _ _ _

1

ALABAMA

OBJECTIVES: To improve knowledge of geographical facts about Alabama.

To improve research skills.

To encourage use of tools that promote career awareness.

MATERIALS: Any encyclopedia.

PROCEDURE:
1. Do the word search.

2. Locate the cities and rivers on the blank map found on the following page.

3. Devise little symbols for the various products and minerals listed and add them to the map.

4. Pick one of the famous men listed and write a biographical report of his life. Be sure to include how it affected the state.

5. By studying the products of the state, what kinds of careers would be most feasible?

6. When our country was young, many shipping firms put out brochures to encourage people to come to America. Do the same for Alabama. Be sure to list the many opportunities for profitable careers that are available.

7. The city of Enterprise has a statue to a bug. Research this. Prepare a report to share with the class about it. Pretend you're a reporter. Tell how, when, where, and why the statue is there.

8. Alabama has two other nicknames. Find them and its motto. Then explain why you think they are appropriate or not.

ALABAMA

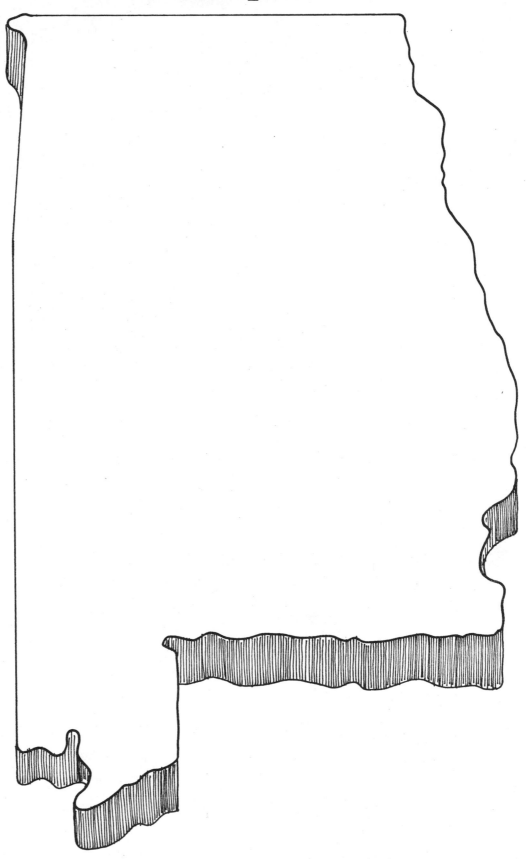

ALASKA

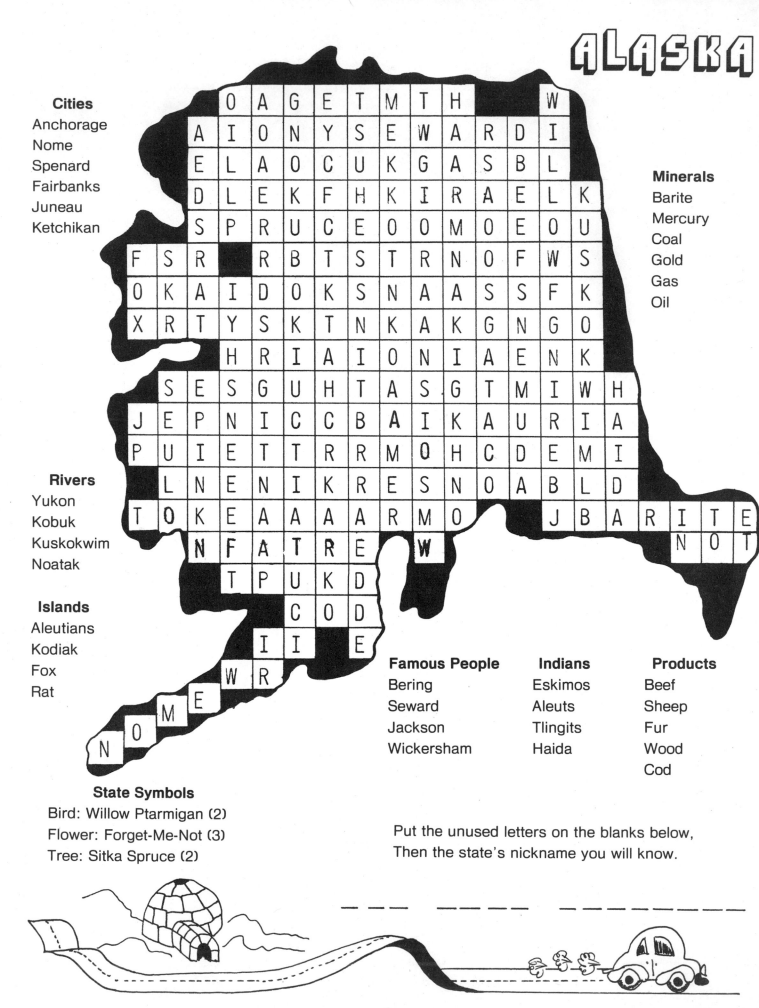

Cities
Anchorage
Nome
Spenard
Fairbanks
Juneau
Ketchikan

Minerals
Barite
Mercury
Coal
Gold
Gas
Oil

Rivers
Yukon
Kobuk
Kuskokwim
Noatak

Islands
Aleutians
Kodiak
Fox
Rat

Famous People
Bering
Seward
Jackson
Wickersham

Indians
Eskimos
Aleuts
Tlingits
Haida

Products
Beef
Sheep
Fur
Wood
Cod

State Symbols
Bird: Willow Ptarmigan (2)
Flower: Forget-Me-Not (3)
Tree: Sitka Spruce (2)

Put the unused letters on the blanks below,
Then the state's nickname you will know.

_ _ _   _ _   _ _ _ _ _ _ _

ALASKA

OBJECTIVES: To encourage students to learn geographical facts about Alaska.

To improve research skills.

To enrich knowledge of glaciers and natural phenomena peculiar to the climate of Alaska.

MATERIALS: Any encyclopedia.

PROCEDURE: 1.   Work the search puzzle and find the nickname.

2.   On the blank map on the next page locate and draw in the cities and rivers listed in the search.

3.   Make a legend for the products and minerals. Put these in where the products are found or the mines are located.

4.   Make a gameboard for you and a friend. Include such things as a blizzard, airplane trouble, fast ice, kayak overturns, sunny weather, sick huskies, tail wind, chased by a bear, and you find new snowshoes. Your destination can be the North Pole or gold. Include any other difficulties or helps you think would apply to Alaska. You can make a circle with numbers as a spinner. Use a paper brad for the spinner itself.

5.   Alaska has "ice that barks." Make an explanation for you to share with your class.

6.   A frozen mastodon was found here. Find out about other prehistoric animals that lived here. Draw them for your class.

7.   Using a shoe box, make a diorama depicting an Eskimo scene.

8.   Alaska has at least two nicknames. Find out what they are and tell why you think they do, or don't, apply.

9.   Research permafrost. Tell what it is and how it affects Alaska.

ALASKA

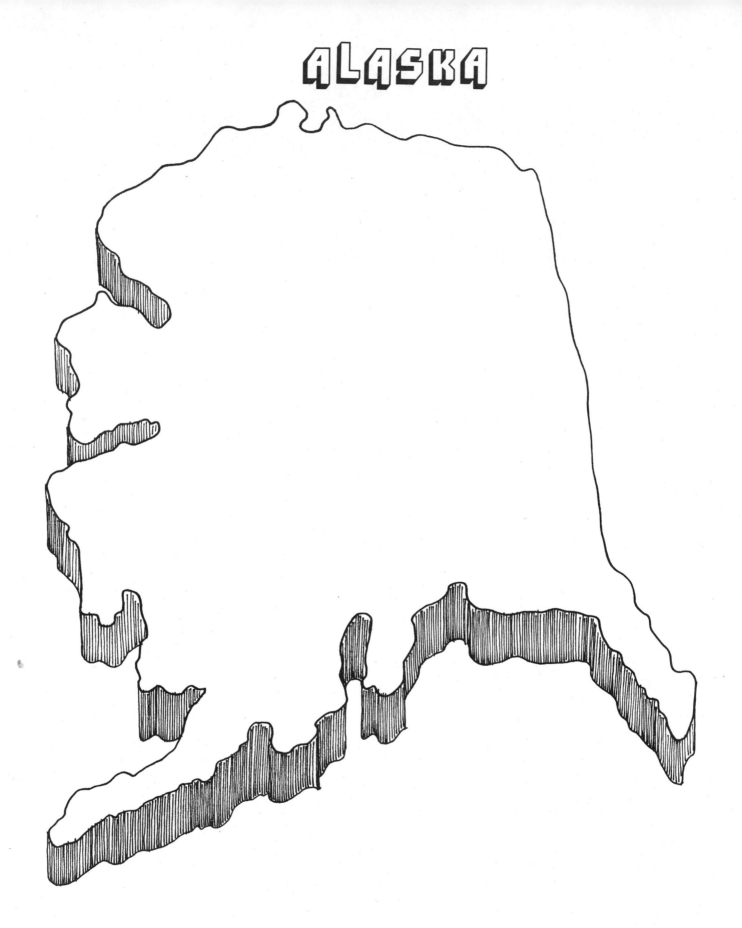

ARIZONA

Cities
- Ajo
- Bisbee
- Flagstaff
- Globe
- Oraibi
- Palo Verde (2)
- Phoenix
- Tempe
- Tombstone
- Tucson

Rivers
- Gila
- Colorado
- Santa Cruz (2)
- San Pedro (2)
- Salt

Minerals
- Copper
- Gold Ore (2)
- Iron
- Lead
- Molybdenum
- Oil
- Petroleum
- Sand

Products
- Beef
- Glass
- Hay
- Machinery

Indians
- Anasazi
- Hohokam
- Mogollon
- Navaho
- Papago
- Pima
- Tonto
- Smoki

Famous People
- Alarcon
- Cochise
- Coronado
- Geronimo
- Poston

Natural Wonders
- Petrified Forest (2)
- Painted Desert (2)
- Grand Canyon (2)

State Symbols
- Bird: (Cactus) Wren
- Flower: Saguaro Cactus (2)
- Tree: Paloverde Palms (2)

Word search grid:

G	L	O	B	E	Y	R	E	N	I	H	C	A	M
R	E	A	T	C	H	N	G	D	L	O	G	B	O
R	F	A	T	R	A	N	O	A	C	S	C	L	I	D	L
N	L	N	R	C	O	S	O	O	Y	H	A	S	A	I	Y
A	A	D	T	E	C	N	L	T	I	S	B	N	O	B	B
S	G	U	A	U	P	O	I	S	S	E	O	S	D	I	D
N	S	L	T	N	R	P	E	M	E	R	M	E	K	A	E
E	T	E	E	A	S	D	O	F	O	L	S	O	H	R	N
R	A	N	D	A	N	R	P	C	A	E	M	O	C	O	U
W	F	O	L	O	D	A	M	P	R	S	P	A	C	N	M
O	F	T	T	E	L	A	M	T	H	I	E	R	Y	O	E
G	O	S	P	O	K	N	S	U	Z	O	A	D	G	R	D
A	O	B	A	O	O	E	C	A	E	L	E	O	R	E	R
P	S	M	H	G	R	H	S	A	A	L	L	N	T	E	E
T	A	I	O	C	O	U	A	A	L	N	L	O	N	I	P	V
P	H	T	F	R	N	A	I	V	O	Y	I	R	M	X	O
A	A	U	G	R	N	A	A	O	E	T	J	L
T	Z	E	O	P	N	T	N	A	E	A
D	E	I	F	I	R	T	E	P

The _ _ _ _ _ _ _ _ _ _ _ _ _ _ _

If your leftover letters you arrange,
You will find the state nickname.

7

ARIZONA

OBJECTIVES: To improve knowledge of geographical facts about the state of Arizona.

To improve research skills.

To promote interest and knowledge of natural phenomena peculiar to Arizona.

To develop an interest and respect for the history of Arizona.

MATERIALS: Any encyclopedia, clay, sand, water and an aquarium.

PROCEDURE:
1. Work the search puzzle and find the state nickname.

2. On the blank map on the following page, locate and draw in the cities listed in the puzzle.

3. Make a little symbol for the various products and minerals listed. Put them in on the blank map.

4. Using clay, make a replica of a Pueblo Indian home.

5. Using clay, make a model of a Spanish Mission.

6. Report on the age of the Grand Canyon. Explain the geological process that formed it. Demonstrate it for your class with sand and water in an aquarium.

7. There are many interesting and different desert plants in Arizona. You might make a folder with plants peculiar to the desert. Start with bear grass, ocotillo, prickly pear, Joshua tree, and saguaro cactus.

8. There are many unusual reptiles in Arizona. Make a pamphlet on them. You might start with the Gila monster, the chuckawalla, the Uta lizard, the king snake, and the horned toad.

ARIZONA

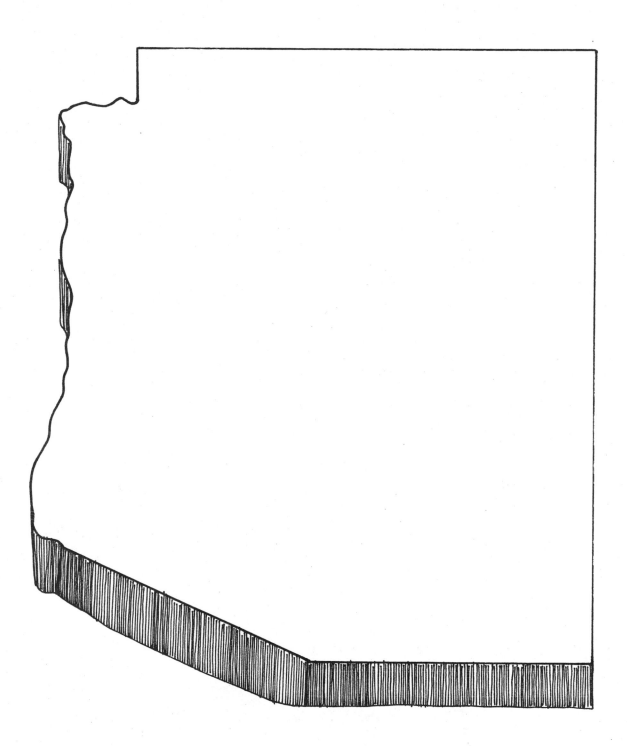

ARKANSAS

Cities
Murfreesboro
Hot Springs
Fort Smith (2)
Fayetteville
Little Rock (2)

Rivers
Arkansas
Mississippi
Sulphur
Red River (2)
White

Indians
Ouachita
Osage
Arikara
Quapaw
Caddo

Minerals
Bauxite
Barite
Bromide
Diamonds
Oil
Gas
Vanodium
Lead

Famous Men
La Salle
De Soto
Marquette
Rose
Fulbright
MacArthur

Products
Lumber
Wheat
Rice
Bean
Hay
Oxen
Beef
Hog
Oat

State Symbols
Bird: Mockingbird
Flower: Apple (Blossom)
Tree: Pine

M	O	N	E	X	O	R	O	B	S	E	E	R	F	R	U	M
P	A	C	W	S	M	T	E	B	R	W	L	A	E	F	H	P
D	I	R	A	H	O	A	A	B	H	O	Y	L	O	V	E	O
R	I	G	Q	S	I	U	C	E	M	E	M	R	A	N	I	E	G
I	E	A	E	U	X	T	A	A	T	U	T	I	I	S	A	R	B
B	S	D	M	I	E	T	E	T	R	H	L	P	D	R	A	E
G	K	G	T	O	I	T	E	L	G	T	R	I	I	E	A	L
N	C	E	N	H	N	V	T	I	T	M	H	K	O	N	T
I	O	U	C	I	I	D	R	E	U	T	A	U	A	N	I
K	R	A	B	L	R	B	S	I	L	R	I	R	R	W
C	U	U	L	A	L	P	D	M	A	P	K	L	A
O	A	E	H	U	R	O	S	R	I	A	P	P
M	A	D	F	P	N	I	O	T	N	T	A	A
D	T	T	D	A	L	S	T	S	O	U	H	G
	Y	V	O	E	U	A	E	Q	H	A	Y
	I	P	P	I	S	S	I	S	S	I	M

Put the unused letters in order and you will have the last word of the state's nickname.

The Land of _____

ARKANSAS

OBJECTIVES: To encourage students to learn geographical facts about Arkansas.

To improve research skills.

To encourage students to explore the geological background of Arkansas.

MATERIALS: Any encyclopedia, salt, flour, cardboard, and watercolors.

PROCEDURE:
1. Do the word search.

2. Locate the cities and rivers on the blank map on the following page. Draw them in place.

3. Develop a legend for the products and minerals and add them to the map on the next page.

4. Using tracing paper, trace the map on plain white paper and paste it on cardboard. Using a mixture of twice as much flour as salt, add a small amount of water to the mixture. Work it with your hands until it becomes clay-like. Using the map in the encyclopedia to help you, mold in the mountains and rivers for the state. Let it dry at least a day, then paint it with watercolors. Label the mountains, plains, and rivers. Put in the cities and anything else to enhance it.

5. Cliff Dweller Indians were among the first to live in Arkansas. Make a mobile showing their tools, homes, food, and weapons.

6. Bauxite is the ore used to make aluminum. Arkansas has large deposits of it. Prepare a report for your class describing the way it is mined and shipped to factories, or use a series of posters to show the steps needed.

7. Arkansas has the only diamond mine in the Western Hemisphere. Make a brochure inviting people to visit the state park where it is found.

8. Arkansas has an interesting rice industry. Prepare a display for the bulletin board about it.

ARKANSAS

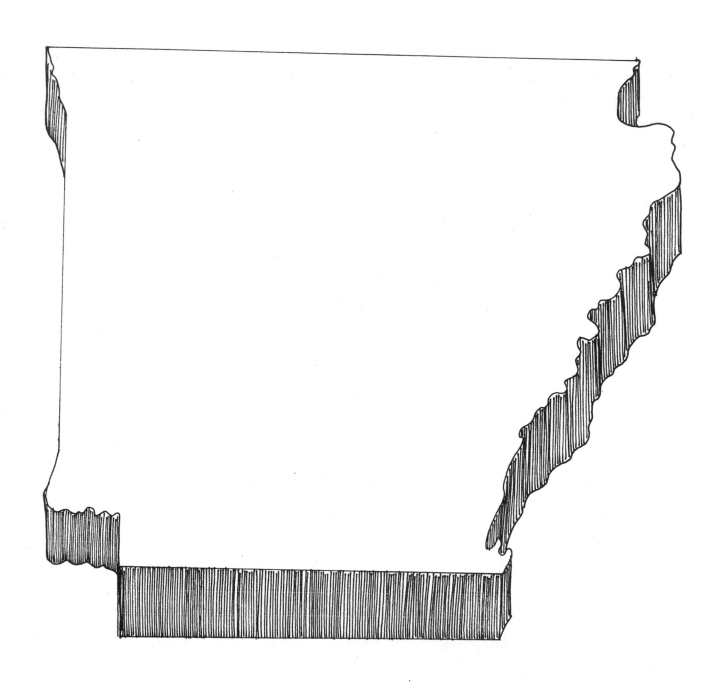

CALIFORNIA

S	A	N	N	A	U	J	O
A	R	A	U	Y	U	M	A
N	E	S	A	T	O	N	K
D	A	H	U	P	A	I	L
I	G	R	T	H	G	X	A.
E	A	L	E	A	D	O	N
G	N	I	P	D	M	N	D
O	M	A	O	L	W	A	P
F	L	L	I	U	O	L	S
R	N	P	P	M	O	K	A
E	E	P	R	D	B	D	C
Y	M	A	I	N	E	O	O	R
L	I	O	O	A	D	R	E	L	A
S	R	N	O	N	K	N	Y	L	M
I	E	M	T	A	U	E	E	O	I	E
E	L	R	C	N	T	J	T	G	R	N
F	D	E	S	O	A	N	N	S	O	B	T
I	I	G	V	L	A	I	M	G	G	A	O
D	G	E	N	R	O	E	U	O	N	L	C
O	A	L	R	L	Q	I	U	F
G	A	S	D	A	A	A	E	T
O	U	D	E	O	E
Q	L	B	O	N	J

Cities
Oakland
Sacramento
San Diego
Anaheim
San Juan (2)
Los Angeles

Indians
Hupa
Pomo
Modoc
Yuma

Rivers
Mojave
Klamath
Colorado
San Joaquin (2)

Products
Airplane
Orange
Lemon
Fig
Tuna
Hay
Beef
Jet
Wine
Plum
Lumber
Nut

Famous Men
Reagan
Nixon
Cabrillo
Disney
Fremont
Drake

Minerals
Tungsten
Lead
Gold
Gas
Oil
Iron
Soda Ash (2)

State Symbols
Bird: (California Valley) Quail
Flower: (Golden) Poppy
Tree: (California) Redwood

Come try your hand,
It's lots of fun.
You'll have the state's nickname
When you're done.
Put the unused letters
On the blanks below.
Be sure they're in order,
Then you'll know.

The _ _ _ _ _ _ State

CALIFORNIA

OBJECTIVES: To encourage students to learn geographical facts about California.

To improve research skills.

To generate historical knowledge and reinforce it.

MATERIALS: Encyclopedia, shoe box, pipe cleaners, old handkerchief, two Popsicle sticks, and glue.

PROCEDURE: 1.   Do the puzzle. Find the nickname.

2.   On the blank state which follows this page, locate the listed cities and the rivers.

3.   Make a legend for the minerals found as well as the products named.

4.   Make a Conestoga wagon. Use the bottom of a shoe box for the base. Use the pipe cleaners for the ribs of the wagon. Glue the handkerchief over the top. Make the wheels out of cardboard. Attach the Popsicle sticks for the horses. Embellish it any way you choose.

5.   The Indians here were not warlike, as they were in the East. Analyze the differences. Illustrate a scene showing one of the tribe's life styles. Include weapons, food, shelter and their forms of transportation.

6.   Make a time line for one of the prominent citizens of California. Speculate on his/her qualities of greatness. Are there others from here who shared these?

7.   Pretend you are a reporter. Interview an old prospector. Relate his hardships as well as his successes. Don't forget the how, when, where, and why questions.

8.   Copy the outline of the state on another sheet of paper. See if you can give it a face or a character of an animal.

CALIFORNIA

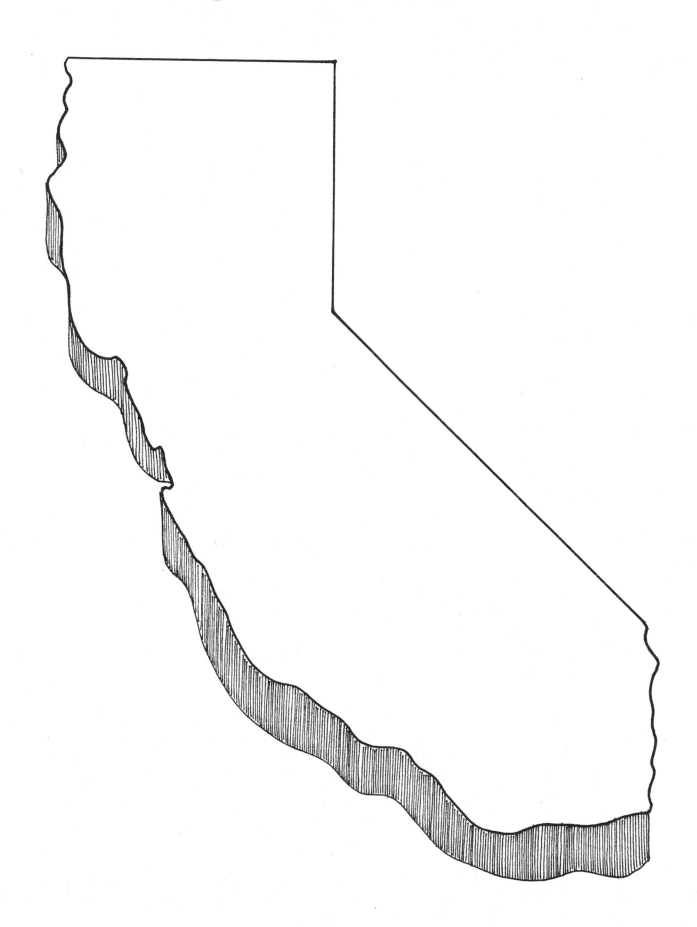

COLORADO

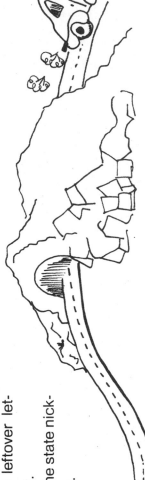

```
M L T D O W N E L G E N I B M U L O C
O T E N U H O I N A S H U T E E B O H
U G Y A I R E A I A G O F C T V B L U E
N E R T D M A T P N R F C T A E O S N Y
T P E E V N N I A G A R R S H T E
A E A E U I R G L R L G E A A E E P N
I R K W B L P L O O P A T D N E E K N
N E K I N S E N L B N O U H Y T P R E
R P I A P E O Y O E E R A C R R K E A D
E P A R N L E U L P A W N G O A V C L N
N C O B I D A U I M O E O I L N O A
E C A E O C S K O L U T S E I D Z U G
D Z Y R E N I H C A M U N E D B Y L O M
```

Cities
Denver
Glenwood Springs (2)
Durango
Greeley
Boulder
Leadville

Rivers
Arkansas
Rio Grande (2)
Colorado
White
(South) Platte

Indians
Kiowa
Arapaho
Cheyenne
Comanche
Pawnee
Utes

Minerals
Petroleum
Molybdenum
Uranium
Silver
Gold
Copper
Coal
Gravel
Zinc
Oil
Gas

Products
Sugar Beet (2)
Machinery
Mint
Sheep
Corn
Rye
Pear
Oat
Grain

Famous Men
Zebulon Pike (2)
Buffalo Bill (2)
Meeker
Carpenter
Long

State Symbols
Bird: Lark Bunting (2)
Flower: Rocky Mountain Columbine (3)
Tree: Blue Spruce (2)

Please put the leftover letters all in a row. When you do, the state nickname will show.

COLORADO

OBJECTIVES: To encourage students to learn geographical facts about Colorado.

To improve research skills.

To encourage students to examine natural phenomena.

To promote use of tools that promote career awareness.

MATERIALS: Encyclopedia, old magazines, glue, and scissors.

PROCEDURE:

1. Work the puzzle. Find the nickname.

2. On the blank state on the following page, locate the cities and rivers listed.

3. Put in the national parks and mountains. Please label the mountain ranges.

4. Make a legend for the products and minerals. Add these to your map.

5. On a blank piece of paper, trace the shape of the state. Using the old magazines, cut out pictures that would pertain to Colorado and its industries and products.

6. Make a brochure to interest people in visiting Colorado and its beauty.

7. Report on the method of mining used for one of the minerals found in this state.

8. Compare the two tunnels dug in this state. Explain their uses and methods of excavation.

COLORADO

CONNECTICUT

Word Search Grid

```
N E W H A V E N H G U A B E N I U Q E
S A R E T P O C I L E H R L E N S P L P
D U M I C A L U B G T I A W E H U O E D
R G B A V O N E O T D H L L E R B Q R R
O A T S C B A I R G A O L R Y S U E N O
F T M K L R K E E Y N U M S T O T A K F
M U S O I U E P R D B A G E T S G C L T
A C C N A N O U O M N G R E Y E L G I R
T K G S I R B N U R E K O O H O J N M A
S S S G T R N R O C C I N O T A S U O H
C O N N E C T I C U T T M H S A N D
Y E N T I H W
C L A Y E L I
O A W T N
B A L L S
K E
```

Cities

Avon
Hartford
Waterbury
New Haven
Bridgeport
Stamford
New London

Rivers

Connecticut
Housatonic
Naugatuck
Quinebaug

Indians

Mohegan
Pequot
Saukiog

Minerals

Clay
Sand
Mica

Famous People

Sherman
Eli Whitney (2)
Block
Hooker
Trumbull
Hale

State Symbols

Bird: Robin
Flower: (Mountain) Laurel
Tree: White Oak Tree (3)

Products

Lobster
Ball Bearings (2)
Tins
Corn
Engine
Cloth
Oyster
Syrup
Helicopter
Subs
Hay
Milk
Eggs
Jets
Clocks
Hens
Oats

If you put the unused letters in order, you will have the state's nickname.

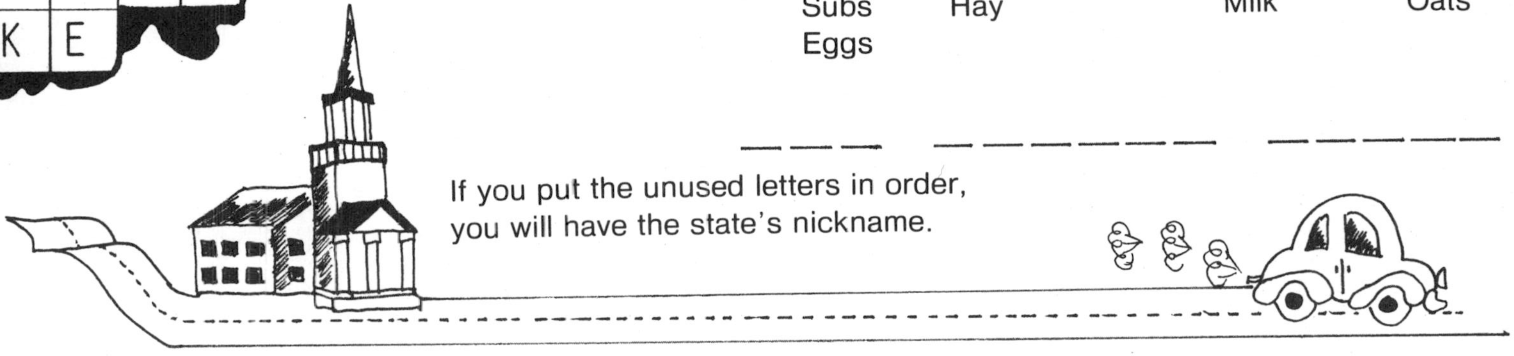

19

CONNECTICUT

OBJECTIVES: To improve geographical knowledge of Connecticut.

To encourage research skills.

To increase historical knowledge of Connecticut.

To encourage student interest in natural phenomena peculiar to Connecticut.

MATERIALS: Encyclopedia, string, scissors, glue, old magazines, cardboard and clay.

PROCEDURE:
1. Work the puzzle. Find the nickname.

2. On the next page, put in the cities and rivers named in the puzzle.

3. On the blank state please put in symbols representing the products and minerals named.

4. Make a mobile with old magazine pictures pasted on cardboard, or draw something a "Yankee Peddler" might have carried on his back or sold from his wagon.

5. Illustrate how you feel a typical scene would have looked in November in the camp of the Pequot Indians. Do another one of the Saukiog camp. List the differences and the similarities.

6. Plan a skit with a friend depicting an incident in the life of one of the men listed in the famous people list from the puzzle.

7. Repeat the story of shaded-tobacco. Explain how it happened and give the reasons it is worth all the effort.

8. The *Nautilus* was the first nuclear submarine. Make a small model of clay and tell its story.

CONNECTICUT

DELAWARE

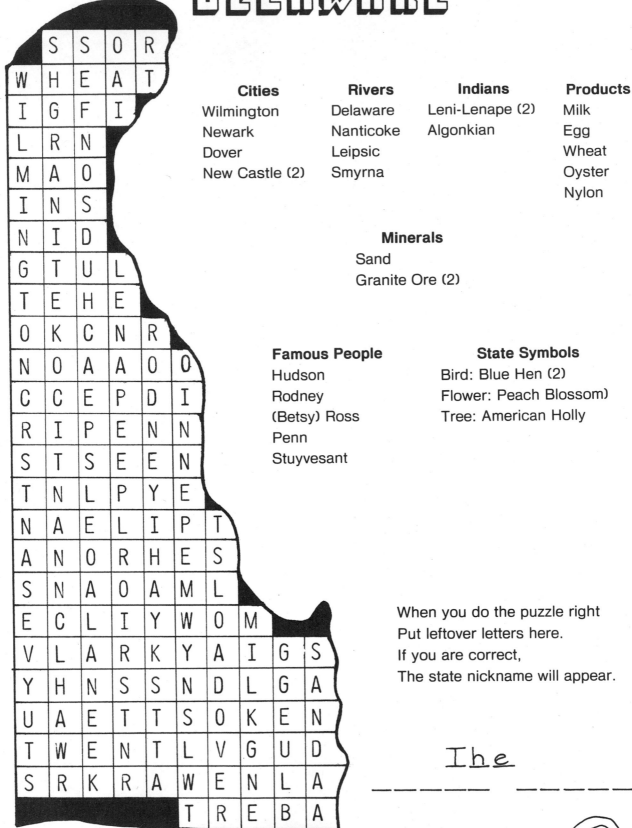

Cities
Wilmington
Newark
Dover
New Castle (2)

Rivers
Delaware
Nanticoke
Leipsic
Smyrna

Indians
Leni-Lenape (2)
Algonkian

Products
Milk
Egg
Wheat
Oyster
Nylon

Minerals
Sand
Granite Ore (2)

Famous People
Hudson
Rodney
(Betsy) Ross
Penn
Stuyvesant

State Symbols
Bird: Blue Hen (2)
Flower: Peach Blossom)
Tree: American Holly

When you do the puzzle right
Put leftover letters here.
If you are correct,
The state nickname will appear.

The ___

_____ _____

DELAWARE

OBJECTIVES: To increase geographical knowledge of the state of Delaware.

To improve research skills.

To encourage historical knowledge of the state of Delaware.

MATERIALS: An encyclopedia, Popsicle sticks, toothpicks, clay, glue, wallpaper, and shoe box.

PROCEDURE: 1.   Do the word search. Find the nickname.

2.   Put in the cities and rivers on the blank map on the following page.

3.   Using a legend, locate the places the products and the minerals are found.

4.   Using the Popsicle sticks, toothpicks and clay, make a model of a settler's home in early Delaware.

5.   Research the story of the Blue Hen Roosters. Using the shoe box, make a diorama about them. You can use wallpaper for the background and make the figures out of clay.

6.   Track down the history of our flag. Prepare a chart showing the different forms of it until now. Be prepared to share with your class the story of Betsy Ross and George Washington.

7.   Probe into the history of this state. Check out the rumor that there was an Egyptian "Columbus" who landed here.

8.   Analyze the climate. Consider how it would affect the people living there. Do the same for the topography.

DELAWARE

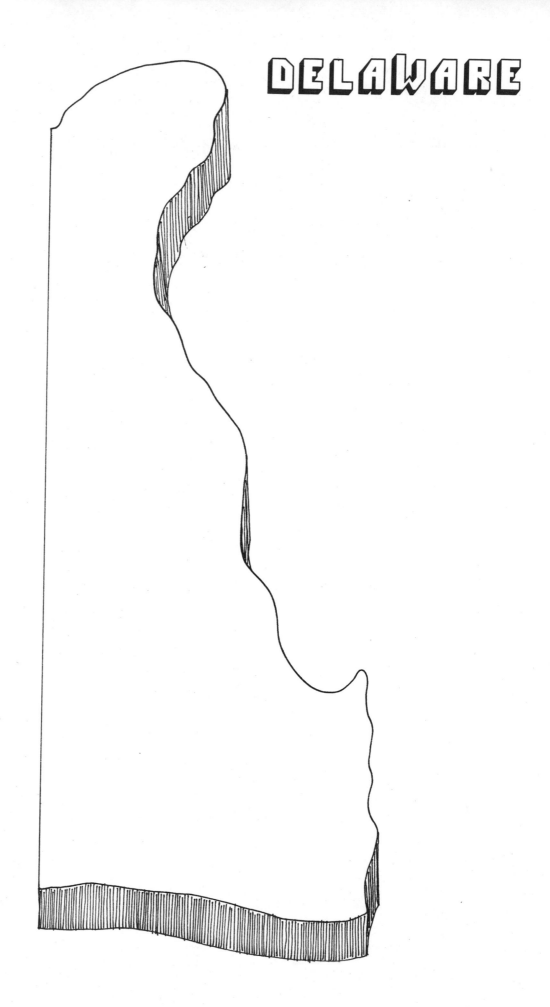

FLORIDA

A	T	O	S	A	R	A	S					
T	A	M	P	A	L	O	C	I	H	C	A	L	A	P	A
T	A	L	L	A	H	A	S	S	E	E	S	P	E	C	A	N
E	T	A	H	P	S	O	H	P	E	A	N	U	T	S	O	U
			Z	E	A	V	R	A	N	N	A	S	J	S
			H	I	M	A	I	M	P	I	U	A	O

N	O	D	E	M	C	N	H
E	C	A	N	K	U	D	N
A	R	K	C	S	N	M	E	S
Y	P	L	I	O	A	G	I	E
S	A	A	A	L	N	N	C	L	T
Y	T	Y	L	A	G	E	O	L
N	S	R	A	M	B	I	L	D
O	E	O	C	M	I	I	A
S	N	U	E	H	S	R	A
A	O	Q	N	E	S	D
B	E	E	U	E
Y	A	L	T	S
P	A	L	M
C	L	A	M

Cities
Tampa
Tallahassee
Pensacola
Sarasota
Miami

Famous People
Narváez
Jackson
Disney
Edison
(Ponce de) León

Rivers
Apalachicola
St. Johns (2)
St. Marys (2)

Minerals
Phosphate
Clay
Sand

Products
Nylon
Lemon
Peanuts
Pecan
Lime
Clam

Indians
Calusa
Tequesta
Apalachee
Timucua

State Symbols
Bird: Mockingbird
Flower: Orange (Blossom)
Tree: Sabal Palm (2)

Put the unused letters on the blanks below.

If you are right, the state nickname will show.

The _ _ _ _ _ _ _ _ State

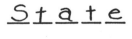

FLORIDA

OBJECTIVES: To improve geographical knowledge of Florida.

To encourage research skills.

To encourage use of tools for career awareness.

To increase historical knowledge of Florida.

MATERIALS: Encyclopedia, paper bag, construction paper, glue, watercolors, scissors, and road maps of U.S.A.

PROCEDURE:
1. Do the word search and find the state nickname.

2. Locate and place on the blank map on the following page the rivers, cities, and the Everglades Swamp.

3. Using a legend, put in the minerals and the products mentioned in the puzzle.

4. Using a large paper bag, design a mask the Indians might have worn for one of their ceremonies. Use construction paper, scissors, glue, and watercolors to make it look authentic.

5. La Fitte was a pirate. Discover how his life story fits in with the history of Florida. Make a report to share with your class.

6. Plan a trip for you and your family to Disney World. Don't forget to save time to visit Epcot. Choose the best route for you and don't forget to plan how far you will travel each day. Estimate the amount of money you'll need and how much gas you'll use.

7. Sink holes have been appearing in central Florida. Find out all you can about them. Devise precautionary measures. Make some posters warning of the dangers from these.

8. Report on an animal or bird that is found only in Florida.

FLORIDA

GEORGIA

H	A	N	N	A	V	A	S		
O	C	T	B	Y	E	E	S	R	
C	K	A	E	M	E	P	T	U	E
C	A	E	E	X	I	N	D	O	B	T
A	O	E	F	P	T	E	T	U	W	M	R
B	L	E	R	E	S	I	I	I	R	A	U	A
O	I	H	E	O	N	L	L	E	H	E	H	L	C
T	N	C	T	P	D	O	H	E	A	W	I	L	O
M	O	A	E	O	S	K	H	S	V	A	E	G	C
S	O	R	N	A	O	A	E	E	Y	T	H	L	O
B	H	U	R	O	M	H	E	E	A	U	C	E	T	S
M	A	H	N	A	O	K	O	T	L	N	T	T	T	A
A	T	R	T	D	O	C	N	L	W	A	I	H	O	N
C	T	L	I	R	A	A	H	O	T	E	M	O	N	D
O	A	R	E	T	L	H	R	E	S	P	D	R	A
N	H	H	O	T	E	B	S	O	E	T	L	P
	C	Y	A	M	A	C	R	A	W	L	O	E
		E	N	O	D	R	O	G
			W	E

Cities
Savannah
Columbus
Macon
Atlanta
Rome
Hull

Minerals
Barite
Kaolin
Gold
Clay
Sand

Famous People
Low
Mitchell
Whitney
De Soto
Gordon
Oglethorpe
Carter

Products
Textiles
Tobacco
Cotton
Peach
Yam
Peanut
Shad
Beef

Rivers
Okefenokee (Swamp)
Altamaha
Canoochee
Chattahoochee
Ohoopee

Indians
Mound Builder (2)
Etowah
Yamacraw

State Symbols
Bird: Brown Thrasher (2)
Flower: Cherokee Rose (2)
Tree: Live Oak (2)

As the leftover letters come into view,
The state's nickname will appear for you.

The _ _ _ _ _ _ _

_of_ _the_ _South_

28

GEORGIA

OBJECTIVES: To encourage students to learn geographical facts about Georgia.

To improve research skills.

To promote historical knowledge about Georgia.

To improve knowledge of swamps and natural phenomena peculiar to freshwater swamps.

MATERIALS: An encyclopedia, clay, poster board, crayons.

PROCEDURE:
1. Work the word search and find the nickname.

2. On the blank map on the following page, locate the cities and draw in the rivers listed in the search.

3. Make a legend for the products and minerals. Draw these in where the products are made and where the mines are located.

4. Eli Whitney invented the cotton gin. Research his life story. Find out what his other great invention was. Make an illustrated report on his life. Explain how his genius affected the Northern part of our country as well as the South.

5. Coca-Cola was invented in Atlanta. Find out why and how it was done. Make a poster advertising it as it was first used.

6. Peanuts are considered nuts, but they are not true nuts. Unearth the true story. Draw their life cycle. Dr. George Washington Carver found many and varied uses for them. Share with your class the many ways he used them.

7. Using clay, make a miniature scene of the swamp. What are the differences between the alligator and the crocodile? How is the alligator essential to the ecology of the swamp? Who are its enemies?

8. Kaolin is a special kind of clay. Investigate its uses and how it is processed.

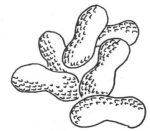

GEORGIA

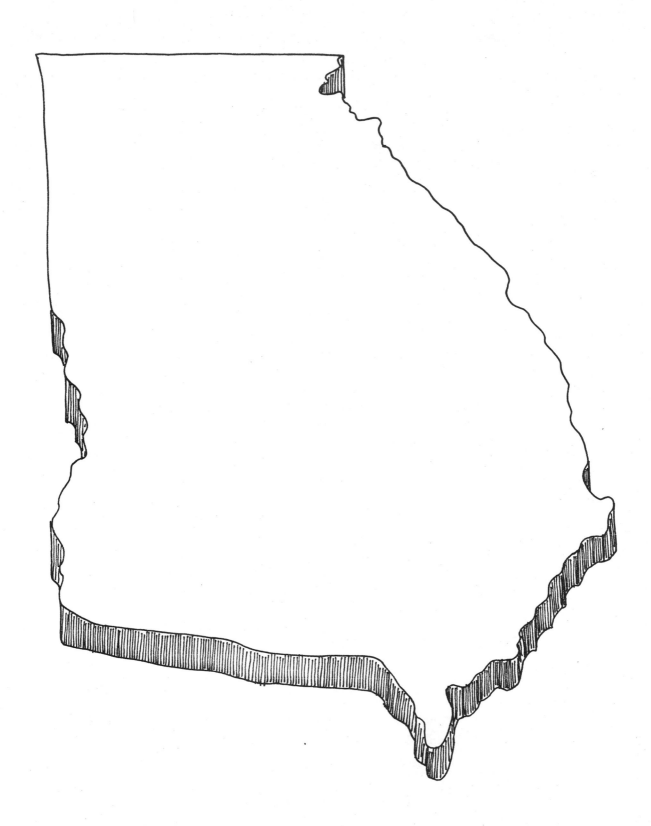

HAWAII

Famous People
Cook
Burns
Kamehameha

Islands
Oahu
Hawaii
Niihau
Maui
Lanai
Kahoolawe

Cities
Hilo
Honolulu
Paia
Ewa
Hana
Koele
Aiea
Kailua
Pearl Harbor (2)

Products
Whale   Beef
Fish   Bee
Tuna   Sugar Cane (2)
Eggs   Pineapple
Coffee   Hogs
Corn

State Symbols
Bird: (Nene) Hawaiian Goose (2)
Flower: Hibiscus
Tree: Kukui

Put the unused letters on the blanks below.
If you are right, the state nickname will show.

___ ___ ___   ___ ___ ___ ___ ___ ___ ___

HAWAII

OBJECTIVES: To encourage students to learn geographical facts about the state of Hawaii.

To improve research skills.

To develop an interest in the natural beauty and structure of the Hawaiian Islands, including knowledge of volcanoes.

To research the cultural background of Hawaii, including the six races found there.

MATERIALS: An encyclopedia, newspaper, toothpicks, Popsicle sticks, glue, scissors and crayons.

PROCEDURE:
1. Do the word search and find the nickname.

2. Devise little symbols for the various products and minerals. Using a legend, put them on the map on the next page.

3. Using the list as your guide, put in the cities.

4. Find out why the Hawaiians use the kind of boat they do. Using newspapers and glue, make one. Use toothpicks and Popsicle sticks to make it more realistic.

5. Using paper-mache, which is glue and paper, make a small volcano. See if you can find out why Mt. St. Helens is called a volcano even though it didn't emit any lava. What are the kinds of rocks found in the mountains in Hawaii?

6. On a large piece of cardboard draw in the rest of the islands. They're named on the word search. Shape the mountain ridges on each island. Compare them. How are they alike? How are they different?

7. There are six different races in Hawaii. Please name them. Trace the historical background of how each came to be found in the islands.

8. Pick a plant or animal that is found only in Hawaii. Make a poster showing its life story.

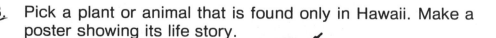

HAWAII

IDAHO

Cities
Boise
Lewiston
Pocatello
Coeur d' Alene
Kellogg
Star

Rivers
Snake
Salmon
Columbia
Deer
Red (Rock)
Elk
Bear

Minerals
Silver
Gold
Lead
Phosphate

Famous People
Clark
Pierce
Thompson
Spalding
(Chief) Joseph

Indians
Nez Perce (2)
Bannock
Shoshoni
Kutenai

Products
Sheep
Beef
Potato
Pulp
Hens
Hay
Wool

State Symbols
Bird: (Mountain) Bluebird
Flower: (Mock) Orange
Tree: (Western White) Pine

Put the leftover letters on the blanks below.
If you're correct, the state nickname will show.

____ ____ ____

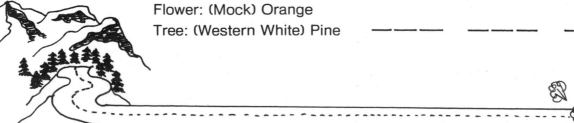

IDAHO

OBJECTIVES: To improve geographical knowledge about Idaho.

To improve research skills.

To encourage use of tools that promote career awareness.

MATERIALS: Any encyclopedia, cardboard, glue, watercolors, clay, and macaroni.

PROCEDURE:

1. Do the word search and find the nickname.

2. On the next page is a blank map. Please put in the cities and rivers named.

3. Make a legend for the products and minerals. Draw them in where they are produced or mined.

4. What kinds of careers do you think would make a good living in Idaho? Make a brochure to lure trained people for the particular field you are interested in. For instance, geologists, farmers, or engineers might be interested in moving here.

5. Place a piece of paper over the blank map on the next page. Trace the shape of the state. Paste it on cardboard and glue macaroni on where the mountains are. When it is dry, paint it. Draw in the rivers in blue. Add clay where the mountains aren't so high.

6. Research Chief Joseph. He was a great influence on the people of Idaho. Make a report to share with your class on his life story. Do you think he was a good chief or not? Why?

7. Idaho has a peculiar shape. Can you make something else out of it? Make a rebus for your class for the bulletin board. You can start with an eye, add the letters D and A, then draw in a hoe.

8. The seal of Idaho portrays what the people think are the most important occupations. Reproduce the seal; then list the reasons for the symbols.

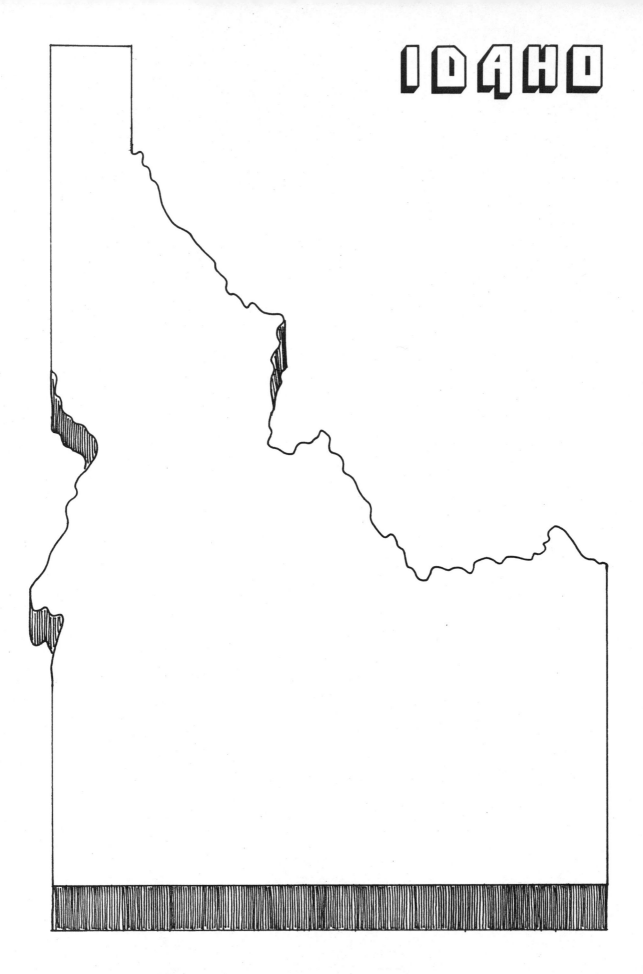

IDAHO

ILLINOIS

Cities
Chicago
Springfield
Peoria
Wilmette
Rockford

Rivers
Mississippi
Rock
Ohio
Illinois

Products
Potatoes	Wood
Wool	Glue
Corn	Hogs
Peach	Wheat
Oats	Milk
Pea	Hay

Minerals
Coal
Fluorite
Tripoli
Gas
Iron

Indians
Winnebago
Tamaroa
Iroquois
Chippewa
Sauk
Kickapoo
Shawnee
Potawatomi
Cahokia

Famous People
Lincoln
Grant
Clark

State Symbols
Bird: Cardinal
Flower: (Native) Violet
Tree: (White) Oak

O	G	A	C	I	H	C	N	M	
O	A	T	S	S	R	R	I		
	P	E	H	T	O	O	S	D	
	E	O	A	H	C	C	C	S	L
E	A	T	W	I	K	I	K	W	I	E
C	A	N	L	F	R	C	I	W	S	I
H	T	E	O	O	O	N	N	I	P	S	F
I	O	E	P	R	Q	L	N	L	L	K	I	G
P	R	I	D	U	O	E	M	I	L	L	P	N
R	R	O	O	C	B	E	F	M	I	I	P	I
T	O	I	N	A	T	T	L	O	N	M	I	R
W	S	I	C	T	O	A	U	T	O	T	A	P
L	O	E	T	I	M	O	A	I	E	I	S
A	Y	A	H	A	R	W	S	L	K	A
	P	E	O	R	I	A	L	O	O	U
	H	G	O	T	T	A	I	H	K
	W	S	A	E	O	N	V	A	I
	A	W	E	P	P	I	H	C	R
	C	L	A	R	K	D	G	O
		I	O	A	K	R	L	A
		E	O	A	A	U	L
			N	W	C	E
			T	G	A	S

If you put the unused letters on the blanks below,
the state's nickname you'll come to know.

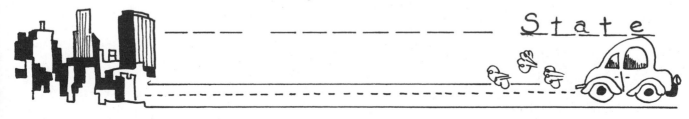

___ _____ State

37

ILLINOIS

OBJECTIVES: To improve geographical knowledge about the state of Illinois.

To encourage political awareness of the state's governmental organization.

To encourage the improvement of research skills.

To promote cultural understanding of problems of big cities.

MATERIALS: Any encyclopedia, cardboard, and a spinner.

PROCEDURE:
1. Do the word search. Find the nickname.

2. Place the listed cities and rivers on the blank map on the following page.

3. Make symbols for the various products and minerals. Add these to the map on the next page.

4. Research the Lincoln-Douglas debates. Explain their importance to our whole country as well as Illinois. Suppose you had been a reporter at one of them. Write up an interview with Mr. Lincoln or Mr. Douglas. Be sure you remember the where, when, why, and how questions.

5. Make a chart showing the structure of the government of Illinois. Show how the three branches of government serve as a check, or balance, for the other two. How often are the representatives, senators, and the governor elected? How are the judges selected?

6. Prepare a gameboard for you and a friend to play. Make the object of your game to find the thief who robbed your friend's father's store. Have stops along the way, such as the thief's cap was found, skip two spaces forward; you lost your notebook of clues, go back to the beginning; hot tip, extra turn; wrong person suspected, lose a turn; you found one of the stolen items in a pawn shop, take an extra turn; and unsuspected reward on the criminal.

7. Analyze two problems found in the inner city of a big city like Chicago that would foster a robbery like you made a game for.

ILLINOIS

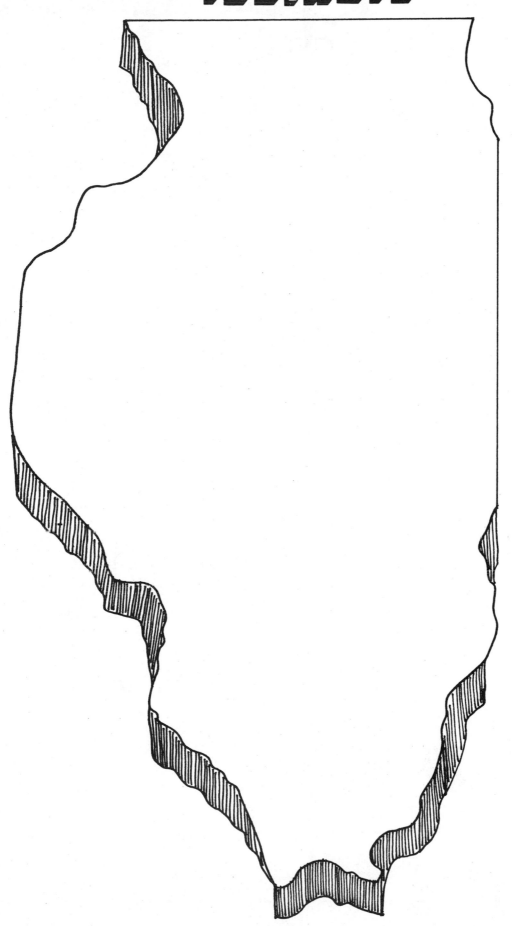

INDIANA

Cities
Evansville
Indianapolis
Gary
Fort Wayne (2)
Kokomo
Lynn
Hall
Amo
Troy
Rome (City)
Cadiz

Minerals
Limestone
Gas
Oil
Clay
Sand
Gravel
Stone
Coal
Iron Ore (2)

Products
Cement
Onions
Lumber
Grain
Wheat
Oat
Glass
Rubber
Yam
Sugar Beet (2)
Snap Beans (2)

Melon
Soybean
Pea
Hogs
Rye
Pear
Corn
Sheep
Hay

Rivers
Wabash
Ohio
White
Eel

Indians
Miami
Wea
Fox
Huron
Sauk

Famous People
Studebaker
Harrison
Ray
Owen

Gatling
Clark
Riley
Ade

State Symbols
Bird: Cardinal
Flower: Peony
Tree: Tulip Tree (2)

L		G	A	S	U	G	A	R	Y	S	B
I	D	I	H	N	N	Y	L	O	T	N	E
O	N	Y	M	I	O	A	R	U	U	A	E
I	A	D	L	A	N	T	D	N	L	P	T
H	S	T	I	I	I	E	Y	O	I	E	W
O	A	E	D	A	B	M	N	L	P	N	A
G	Y	R	L	A	N	O	D	E	T	O	Y
S	A	U	K	L	O	A	E	M	R	T	N
C	M	E	L	M	I	H	P	A	E	S	E
L	R	A	O	G	S	V	E	O	E	E	G
A	H	K	R	C	F	P	S	S	L	M	L
R	O	A	L	O	N	I	O	N	S	I	A
K	I	A	X	E	T	I	H	W	A	L	S
N	Y	I	N	O	N	N	A	H	E	V	S
N	R	O	Y	G	R	A	V	E	L	N	E
O	T	E	S	T	O	E	Z	A	W	W	I
N	S	L	L	N	N	C	B	I	T	A	L	E
	I	T	U	A	E	P	Y	D	B	A
	R	R	O	M	E	M	R	O	A	O
	O	R	U	B	B	E	R	S	C
F	Y	A	R	E	S	C	H	T
E	M	H	U	R	O	N		A
O	T		E

Please put the unused letters on the blanks below.
If you're correct, the state nickname will show.

The _____ _____

40

INDIANA

OBJECTIVES: To improve the geographical knowledge about Indiana.

To improve research skills.

To promote student awareness of transportation history in Indiana.

To encourage student appreciation of literary skills in Indiana.

MATERIALS: An encyclopedia, old magazines, scissors and glue.

PROCEDURE:
1. Do the word search to find the state nickname.

2. On the map on the following page, please put in the cities listed and draw in the rivers named.

3. Using small symbols put in the minerals and products for Indiana.

4. Research the history of the Indianapolis Motor Speedway. Prepare a report for your class as to how the race developed. Be sure to include the benefits all drivers have received from it. With a friend illustrate some of the old cars. Ask if you can place your pictures and report on the bulletin board.

5. Indiana has some literary heroes: James Whitcomb Riley, Lew Wallace, Booth Tarkington, Theodore Dreiser and Edward Eggleston. Find out the most famous work of each of these men. Which one do you prefer? Make a time line of his life story.

6. Using the old magazines, find pictures advertising Indiana products. Trace the shape of the state on a blank piece of paper and paste your pictures on it. Make a collage of its products.

7. The Studebaker brothers had an interesting life. Find out what they did and where they lived. Make two or three models of their products out of clay.

8. Draw the state flag. Explain what the figures on it mean.

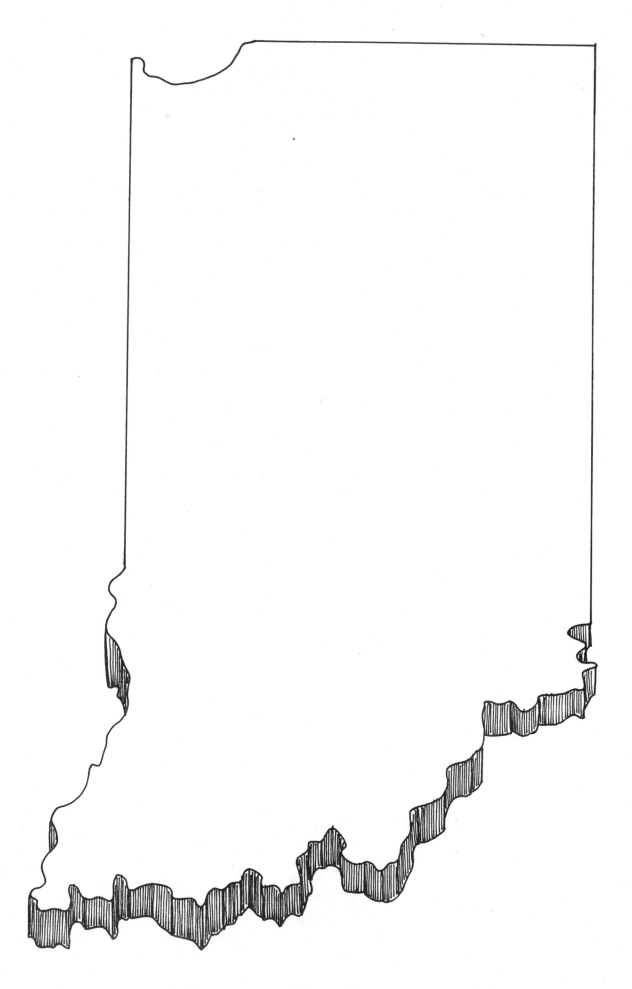

INDIANA

IOWA

State Symbols
Bird: Eastern Goldfinch (2)
Flower: Wild Rose (2)
Tree: Oak

Cities
Ottumwa
Iowa City (2)
Bettendorf
Maquoketa
Waterloo
Council Bluffs (2)
Fort Dodge (2)
Sioux City (2)
Cedar Rapids (2)

Rivers
Mississippi
Wapsipinicon
Missouri
Iowa
Des Moines

Products
Beef	Rye
Melons	Sorghum
Corn	Cattle
Soybean	Potato
Tomato	Turkey
Honey	Hay
Oats	Hog

Famous People
Grinnell
Greeley
Herbert Hoover (2)
Dubuque
Wood

Minerals
Shale
Limestone
Gypsum
Coal
Clay

Indians
Miami
Sauk
Ottawa
Otos
Fox

Come try your hand;
It's lots of fun.
You'll have the state's
nickname
When you're done.

Put the unused letters
on the blanks below;
Be sure they're in order;
Then you'll know.

The ___ ___ ___ ___

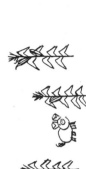

15

IOWA

OBJECTIVES: To improve knowledge of geographical facts about Iowa.

To encourage research skills.

To promote understanding of agricultural facts about Iowa.

To increase historical knowledge of Iowa.

MATERIALS: An encyclopedia, old newspapers, watercolors, scissors, paste, rubber bands, and black yarn.

PROCEDURE: 1.   Do the word search and find the nickname of the state.

2.   Put in the cities and rivers on the blank map on the following page.

3.   Make a legend for the state's products and minerals. Put those on the map as well.

4.   Iowa is well-known for its corn. Take the old newspaper and cut a four-inch strip off the top. Paste it to another four-inch wide strip. Now roll up the newspaper so the edges are like a spiral. Let the tube be about eighteen inches long. Roll it tightly, so it is only about an inch in diameter. Cut four slits in the top of the paper. Pull them down and cut similar slits in two or three places farther on down the tube. You will find it looks like a corn plant.

5.   Using a paper sack, draw an Indian face on one side. Stuff the sack with newspaper. Put a rubber band around the bottom of the bag to hold the newspaper in. Paste the black yarn on the top of the bag like hair. Braid the sides. Cut two small holes for your fingers just above the rubber band on each side. These will be the Indian's arms. Make up a skit and perform it with a friend that tells about something that might have happened in the past to the Indians of Iowa.

6.   Herbert Hoover was the only President from Iowa. Report on his life. Write an essay on whether or not you agree with his policies as President.

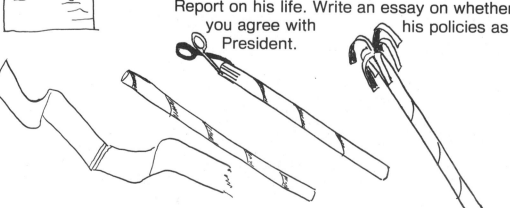

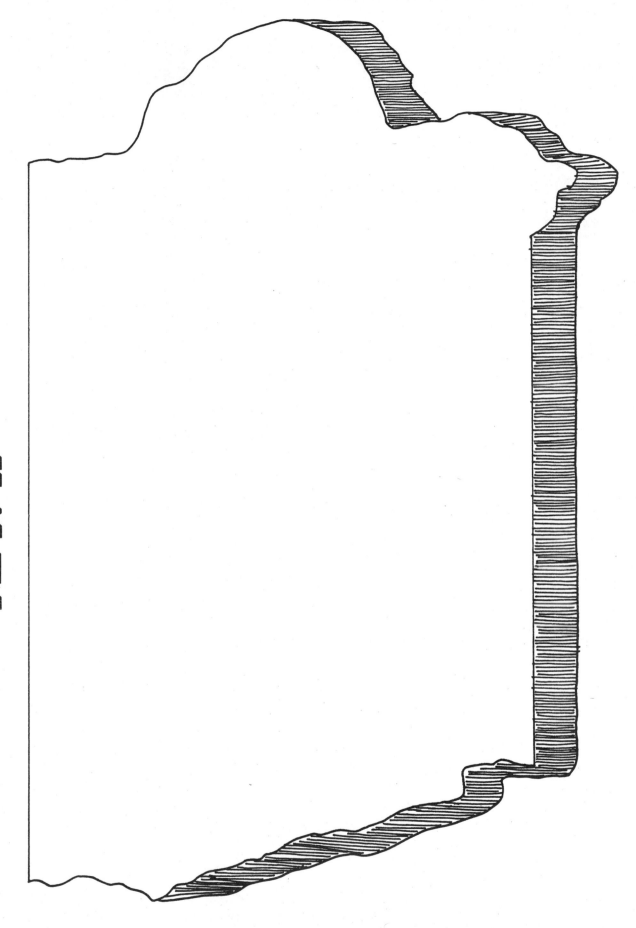

IOWA

KANSAS

R	E	W	O	L	F	N	U	S	H	T	R	O	W	N	E	V	A	E	L	P	S
D	J	E	E	N	W	A	P	C	U	S	T	E	R	H	U	T	N	I	U	O	N
O	E	O	N	S	A	S	N	A	K	R	A	F	C	E	I	E	M	L	T	O	H
O	S	L	H	W	T	N	W	O	R	B	S	N	H	L	E	I	T	L	A	S	A
W	R	A	A	N	E	W	N	E	A	N	C	I	S	C	N	I	Z	W	O	Y	Y
N	O	I	G	W	L	H	R	E	S	M	E	I	B	T	E	O	H	A	P	A	R
O	C	D	L	E	A	O	S	N	O	Y	W	A	O	M	U	I	L	E	H	T	G
T	K	O	A	E	C	R	A	C	E	E	R	N	K	I	C	K	A	P	O	O	H
T	A	D	A	E	Y	K	E	H	O	G	E	S	O	Y	B	E	A	N	S	M	U
O	K	R	A	L	M	A	C	H	I	N	E	R	Y	I	R	U	O	S	S	I	M
C	I	M	A	R	R	O	N	L	E	N	K	C	E	B	W	Y	A	N	D	O	T
E	I	S	E	N	H	O	W	E	R	O	D	A	N	O	R	O	C	T	A	E	H

Cities
Topeka
Abilene
Shawnee
Ada
Wichita

Rivers
Missouri
Arkansas
Kansas
Cimarron

Famous People
Eisenhower
Leavenworth
Custer
Riley
John Brown (2)
Becknell
Coronado

Indians
Pawnee
Arapaho
Cheyenne
Osage
Wyandot
Potawatomi
Kickapoo
Delaware
Comanche

Products
Machinery
Sorghum
Soybeans
Corn
Bees
Hog
Hay
Wheat

Minerals
Helium
Zinc
Lead
Rock Salt (2)
Pumice
Coal
Limestone

State Symbols
Bird: Western Meadow Lark (3)
Flower: Sunflower
Tree: Cottonwood

Put the unused letters in a row.
You'll have the state nickname
on the blanks below.

The _ _ _ _ _ _ _ _ State

46

16

KANSAS

OBJECTIVES: To increase geographical knowledge of the state of Kansas.

To improve research skills.

To promote interest in agricultural facts about Kansas.

To encourage knowledge of career awareness tools.

MATERIALS: An encyclopedia, a shoe box, clay, watercolors, scissors, glue, and pipe cleaners.

PROCEDURE:
1. Do the word search and find the state nickname.

2. Please put the cities and rivers listed in the search on the blank map on the following page.

3. Make a legend for the products and minerals of Kansas. Place them also on the map.

4. Winter wheat is very important to the Kansas economy. Draw three or four stages of the plant, including the approximate dates for its growth. Make a chart to compare it with regular wheat.

5. Using the shoe box, clay, watercolors, glue, and scissors, make a diorama of the Hollenberg Station at Hanover. It is the only pony express station that looks as it did in the 1860's. Use the pipe cleaners for figures.

6. Dwight Eisenhower's boyhood was spent in Abilene. Investigate his life story. With a friend prepare a skit that could have happened to him.

7. Wichita is the leading manufacturing center for small plane parts. Make a mobile showing the various careers necessary to build such a plant.

8. Kansas has two or three nicknames. Find out what they are. Why do you suppose they might or might not apply to this state?

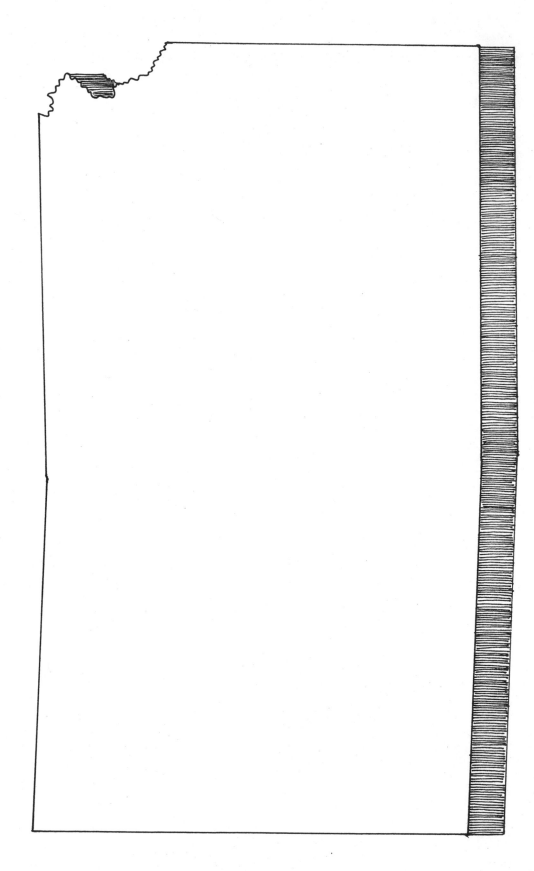

KANSAS

KENTUCKY

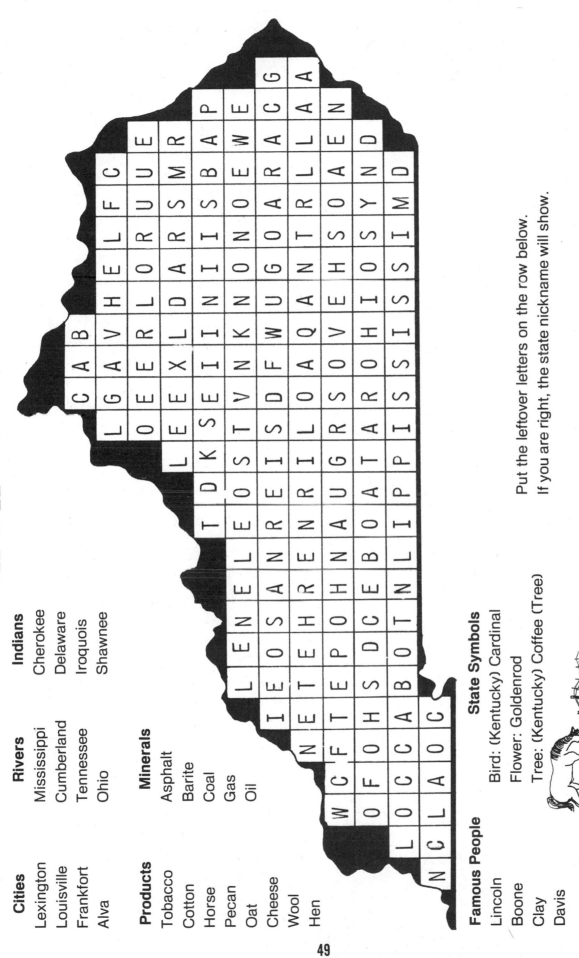

Cities
Lexington
Louisville
Frankfort
Alva

Rivers
Mississippi
Cumberland
Tennessee
Ohio

Indians
Cherokee
Delaware
Iroquois
Shawnee

Products
Tobacco
Cotton
Horse
Pecan
Oat
Cheese
Wool
Hen

Minerals
Asphalt
Barite
Coal
Gas
Oil

State Symbols
Bird: (Kentucky) Cardinal
Flower: Goldenrod
Tree: (Kentucky) Coffee (Tree)

Famous People
Lincoln
Boone
Clay
Davis

Put the leftover letters on the row below.
If you are right, the state nickname will show.

The _____ _____ State

49

17

KENTUCKY

OBJECTIVES: To improve geographical knowledge about the state of Kentucky.

To encourage students to use research skills.

To promote interest in Kentucky's historical past.

MATERIALS: An encyclopedia, Popsicle sticks, and glue.

PROCEDURE:

1. Do the word search and find the state nickname.

2. Put in the listed cities and rivers on the blank state on the following page.

3. Make a legend for the products and minerals for the state. Put them on the map along with the rivers and cities.

4. Kentucky is famous for its horses. The Kentucky Derby is especially well-known. Write a short report on the most famous horse race in the United States.

5. Using the Popsicle sticks and glue, build a model of the cabin in which Abraham Lincoln was born.

6. Daniel Boone was a famous trail finder and settler of this region. With some friends, pantomime an incident that could have happened to him. You'll need to read his life story to find this out.

7. Mammoth Cave is one of the largest in the country. What kinds of minerals are found in it? Where is it located? What kinds of equipment and training would you need to explore such a natural wonder?

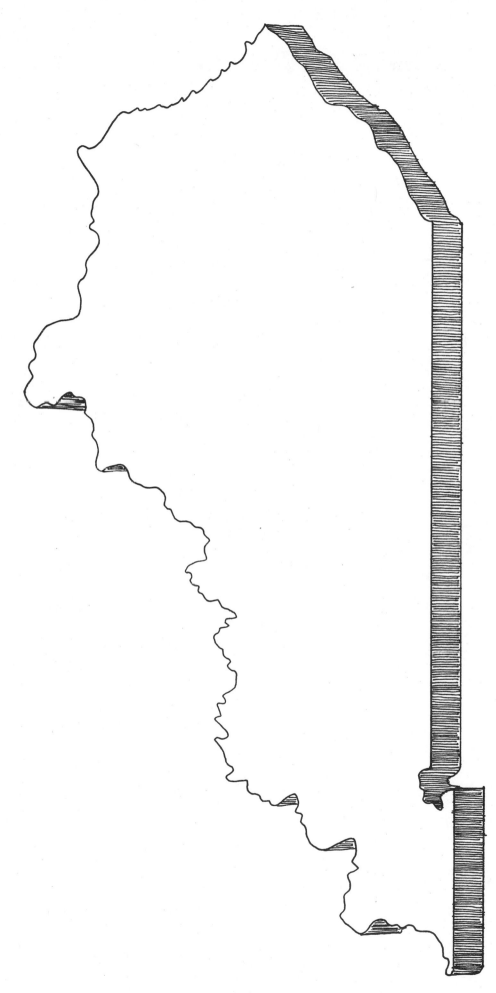

KENTUCKY

LOUISIANA

Cities
New Orleans (2)
Baton Rouge (2)
Shreveport
Bogalusa

Rivers
Mississippi   Sabine
Calcasieu   Ouachita
Pearl   Red

The word search grid contains the following letters:

I	P	P	I	S	S	I	S	S	I	M	E
E	E	R	O	B	G	A	S	N	O	F	G
C	L	P	O	O	A	E	L	U	P	U	U
I	I	L	K	R	R	T	A	T	E	R	O
R	C	R	A	P	L	C	O	I	A	T	R
A	H	Y	S	H	E	S	N	R	L		
N	C	O	I	A	A	A	O	L	E		
	E	T	C	C	L	P	N	E			

R	A	T	L	T	E	A	A	S	U	L	A	G	O	B	
U	L	A	I	V	A	C	P	Z	A	R	A	G	U	S	
F	C	L	E	F	I	W	I	A	E	B	N	H	O	J	O
L	I	R	I	N	F	N	Y	W	K	H	I	O	R	E	D
U	H	S	U	O	C	A	C	A	E	A	C	N	S	O	D	L
S	H	T	E	N	A	C	L	N	L	N	T	T	E	K	A	P
	C	H	I	T	I	M	A	C	H	A	A	W	C	E	
		A	A	I	L	O	N	G	A	M	T	J
		Y	A		N				T	J

Famous People
Jackson
La Salle
Laffite
John Law (2)
Long
Boré

Products
Okra
Rice
Sugar Cane (2)
Nut
Hen
Pea
Yam
Fish
Sod
Fur

Minerals
Oil
Zinc
Salt
Gas
Sulfur Ore (2)
Clay
Peat

Indians
Atakapa
Caddo
Chitimacha
Tunica
Choctaw
Natchez

State Symbols
Bird: (Brown) Pelican
Flower: Magnolia
Tree: (Bald) Cypress

Put the unused letters on the blanks below.
If they're in order, the nickname will show.

The _ _ _ _ _ _ _ State

18

LOUISIANA

OBJECTIVES: To improve knowledge of geographical facts about Louisiana.

To encourage research skills.

To promote interest in Louisiana's historical background.

MATERIALS: An encyclopedia, sand, water, an empty aquarium, paper bag, yarn, glue, crayons, a blank United States map, and clay.

PROCEDURE:

1. Do the word search and find the state nickname.

2. Put the cities and rivers listed in the search on the blank map on the next page.

3. Make a legend including the products and minerals listed in the search. Add these to the map.

4. The Louisiana Purchase changed the shape of our country. Research it. Write a report on it. Who was involved? Why did we buy it? How much land was included? What country did we buy it from? Using the blank United States map, color in the Louisiana Purchase.

5. The Mississippi delta is the largest in our country. Find out why it is there. Using the aquarium, sand and water, demonstrate for your class how it got there. Why is it so fertile? Is it a help or a hindrance to the people there?

6. Laffite had a picturesque influence on this state. Using the paper bag, yarn, and crayons, make a pirate's mask. Then make a model of a pirate ship out of clay. Tell your class all about him and his men.

7. Every year New Orleans has a big parade called the Mardi Gras. Analyze the name, and tell how long it has been used. With another paper bag invent a mask suitable for the celebration. How many visitors does it draw? Is it a help or a hindrance to the economy of New Orleans?

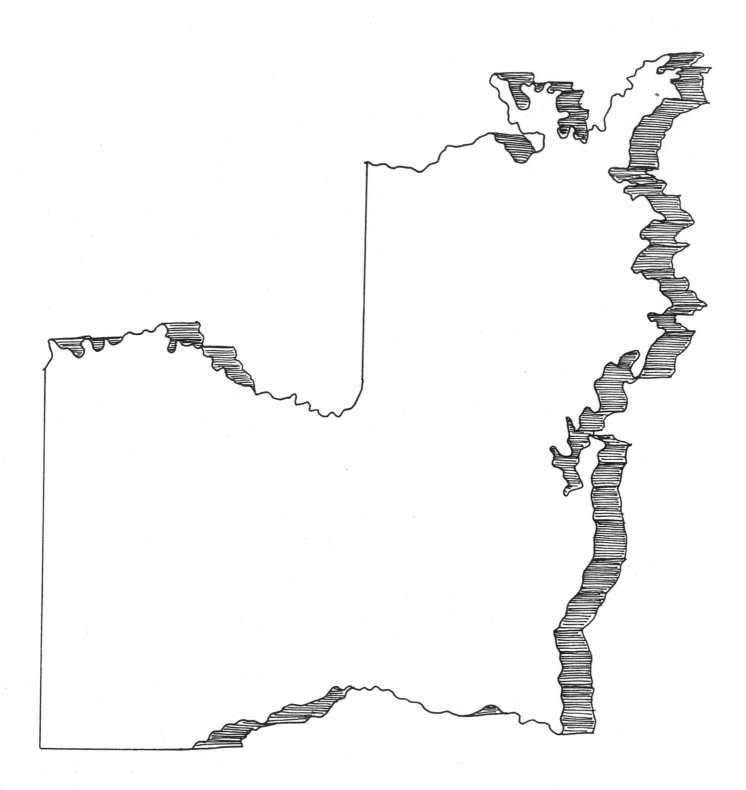

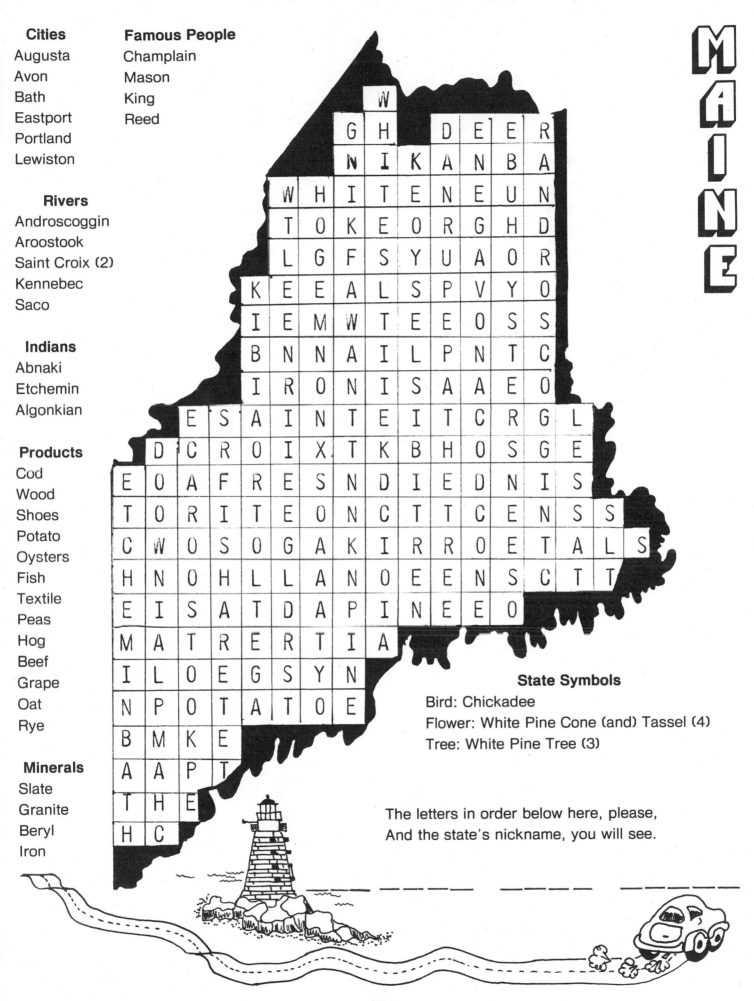

MAINE

Cities
Augusta
Avon
Bath
Eastport
Portland
Lewiston

Famous People
Champlain
Mason
King
Reed

Rivers
Androscoggin
Aroostook
Saint Croix (2)
Kennebec
Saco

Indians
Abnaki
Etchemin
Algonkian

Products
Cod
Wood
Shoes
Potato
Oysters
Fish
Textile
Peas
Hog
Beef
Grape
Oat
Rye

Minerals
Slate
Granite
Beryl
Iron

State Symbols
Bird: Chickadee
Flower: White Pine Cone (and) Tassel (4)
Tree: White Pine Tree (3)

The letters in order below here, please,
And the state's nickname, you will see.

_____ _____

19

MAINE

OBJECTIVES: To improve knowledge of geographical facts about Maine.

To encourage research skills.

To embellish use of career awareness tools.

MATERIALS: An encyclopedia, watercolors and Popsicle sticks.

PROCEDURE: 1.   Do the word search and find the state nickname.

2.   Put the cities and rivers listed in the search on the blank map on the following page.

3.   Make little symbols for the various products and minerals named on the search page. Make a legend for the map and add these to the map on the following page.

4.   Maine has an unusual shape. Trace it on another piece of paper and see if you can make something else from it. Can you see an old salty sea captain?

5.   Maine has more lobsters than any other state. Ferret out its life history. Draw it for your class. What kind of animal is it? Where does it like to live? Describe a "lobster farm."

6.   Maine is a vacation attraction for many tourists. Make a brochure advertising it. What kinds of recreation does it offer?

7.   Maine was the first state to build ships. What does Maine have that would make shipbuilding of long ago profitable? Why do you think they do not build too many ships anymore? Examine the story of the "*Red Jacket*" and the "*Ranger*." See if you can make a model of one of the old ships with Popsicle sticks.

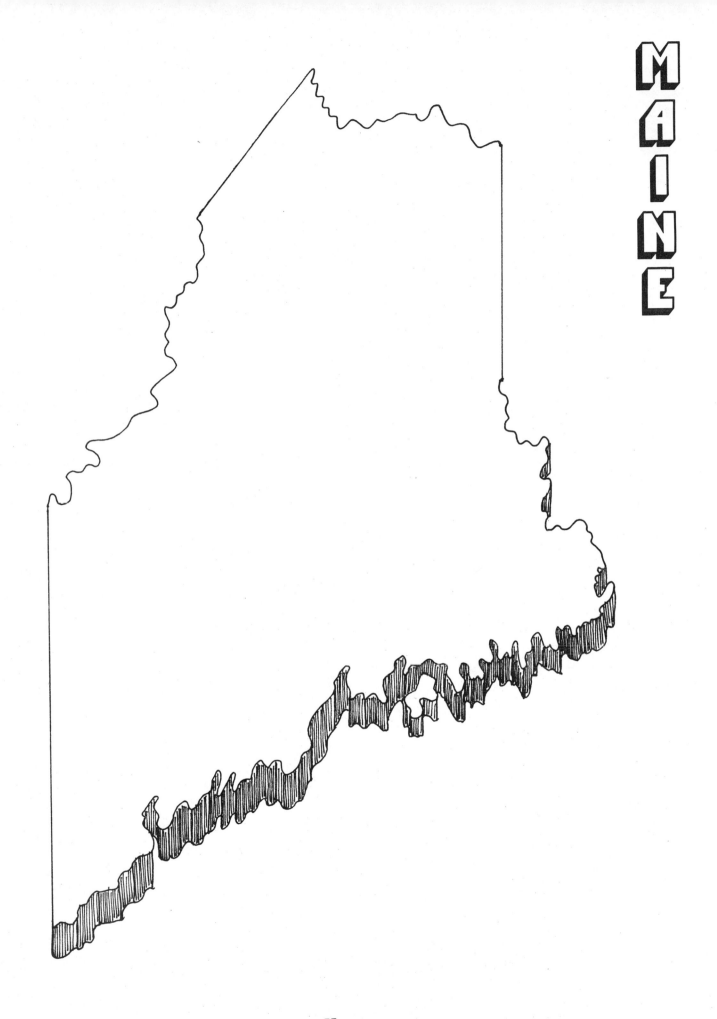

MAINE

MARYLAND

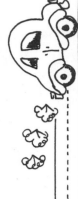

Cities
Washington (D.C.)
Baltimore
Annapolis
Cambridge
Bay (View)

Rivers
Potomac
Chesapeake
Kent Bay (2)
Elk

Famous People
Claiborne
Stone
Taney
Morse
Cooper
Key

Indians
Algonkian
Choptank
Nanticoke

Products
Cotton
Corn
Tobacco
Oyster
Cod
Eel

Minerals
Talc Ore (2)
Sand
Gas
Salt

State Symbols
Bird: (Baltimore) Oriole
Flower: (Black-Eyed) Susan
Tree: White Oak (2)

Please put leftover letters on the blanks below.
If you're correct, the nickname will show.

The __e __ __ __ __ __ __ State

20

MARYLAND

OBJECTIVES: To improve knowledge of geographical facts about Maryland.

To encourage use of research skills.

To promote knowledge of natural phenomena of Maryland.

To arouse interest in Maryland's historical facts.

MATERIALS: An encyclopedia, cardboard, and spinner.

PROCEDURE:

1. Do the word search and find the nickname.

2. Put in the rivers and cities that are listed on the blank map on the following page.

3. Make a legend for the minerals and products listed. Put them on the map, also.

4. George Washington threw a coin across the Potomac River, according to legend. Make a gameboard to share with a friend depicting some of his hardships with his men in the Revolutionary War. Have a few obstacles like ran out of food, stop and lose a turn; came to an old fort, move ahead two spaces; got lost, go back three spaces; found some fresh horses, get an extra turn; road washed out, go back two spaces; found a friendly Indian village, go ahead four spaces. Have Washington start at Mount Vernon and rendezvous with his army.

5. Maryland has more oyster farms than any other state. Research them. Tell how they're run, where they are, and how old the oysters have to be before they can be sold.

6. Sir Frances Scott Key wrote "The Star-Spangled Banner." Write the story to share with your class.

7. Washington, D.C. is located on land donated by Maryland. Why is it not included in any one state? Make a time line showing the history of our nation's capitol.

OH— say! can you see,

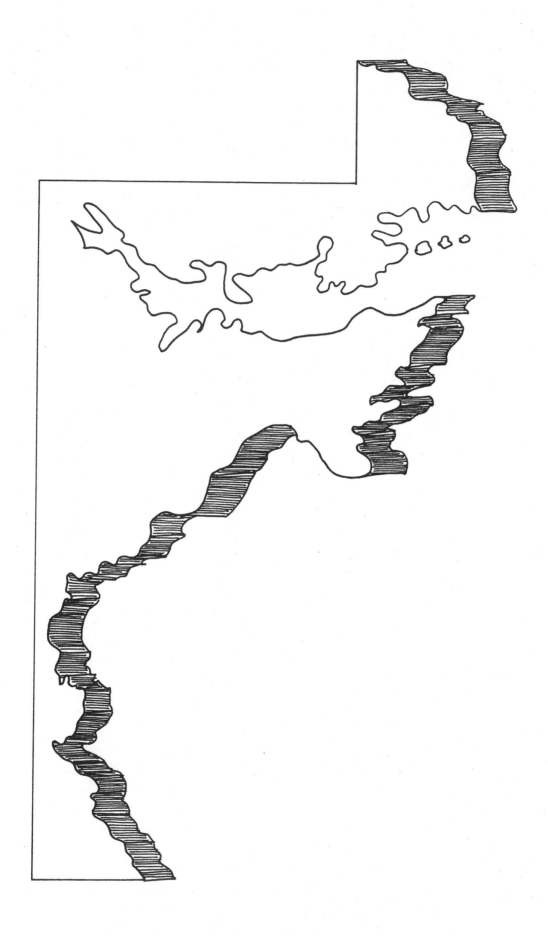

MARYLAND

MASSACHUSETTS

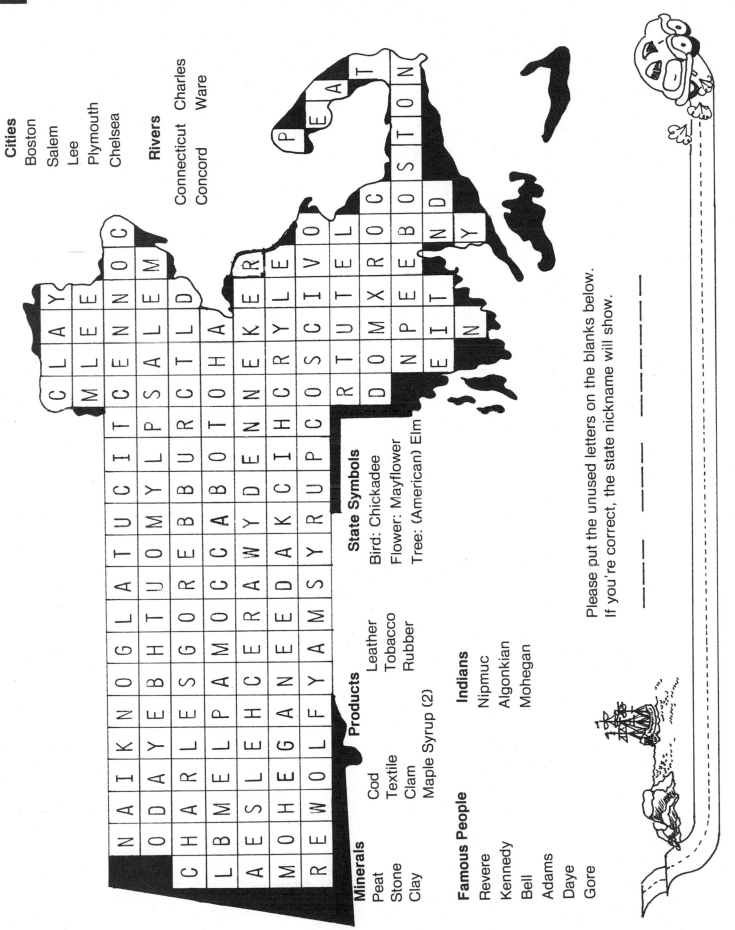

Cities
Boston
Salem
Lee
Plymouth
Chelsea

Rivers
Connecticut Charles
Concord Ware

State Symbols
Bird: Chickadee
Flower: Mayflower
Tree: (American) Elm

Minerals
Peat
Stone
Clay

Products
Cod   Leather
Textile Tobacco
Clam   Rubber
Maple Syrup (2)

Famous People
Revere
Kennedy
Bell
Adams
Daye
Gore

Indians
Nipmuc
Algonkian
Mohegan

Please put the unused letters on the blanks below.
If you're correct, the state nickname will show.

_ _ _ _ _ _ _ _ _ _

21

MASSACHUSETTS

OBJECTIVES: To improve knowledge about Massachusetts' geographical facts.

To encourage research skills.

To promote awareness of Massachusetts' contribution to industrial progress.

MATERIALS: An encyclopedia, shoe box, pipe cleaners, clay, crayons, and scissors.

PROCEDURE:

1.   Do the word search and find the state nickname.

2.   Look up the cities and rivers listed in the search. Put them on the blank map on the following page.

3.   Make a legend for the products and minerals. Put these on the map, also.

4.   Three Presidents have come from Massachusetts. Pick one and write his life story. Tell why you chose him.

5.   Elias Howe, Alexander Graham Bell, and Stephen Daye all did something unique. Pick one, find out what he did, tell how he affected the whole country then, and how he still does today. Make a diorama depicting a scene from your hero's life. Use the shoe box, clay, and pipe cleaners to aid you.

6.   The *Hannah* was the first ship to be in our U.S. Navy. Draw an illustration of her for your class.

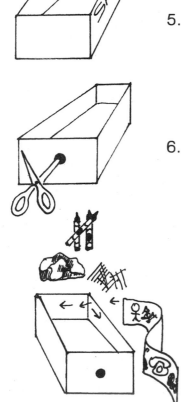

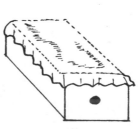

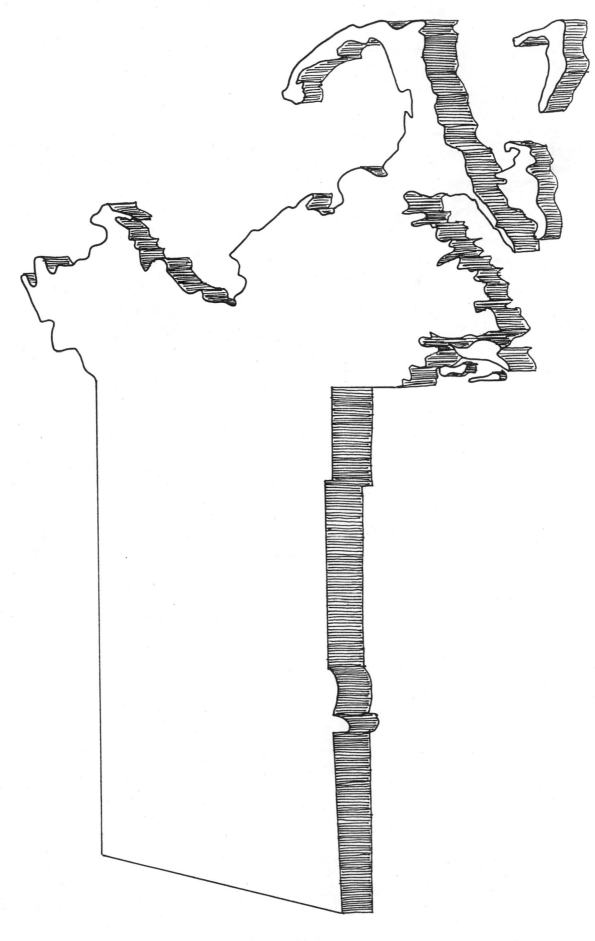

MASSACHUSETTS

MICHIGAN

Indians
Miami
Ottawa

Cities
Lansing
Detroit
Ann Arbor (2)
Battle Creek (2)
Jackson

Rivers
Grand
Kalamazoo
Manistee

Products
Wheat
Chub
Fish
Oil
Cars
Rye

Famous People
Pontiac
Kellogg
Olds
Cadillac

Minerals
Gypsum
Copper
Bromine
Iron Ore (2)
Tar
Salt
Peat

State Symbols
Bird: Robin
Flower: Apple (Blossom)
Tree: White Pine (2)

Put the leftover letters on the blanks below.
If you're right, the state nickname will show.

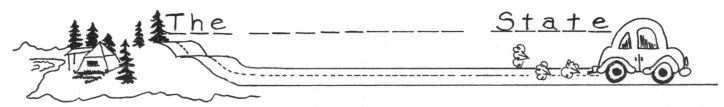

The _ _ _ _ _ _ _ _ _ State

64

22

MICHIGAN

OBJECTIVES: To improve knowledge of geographical facts of Michigan.

To improve research skills.

To promote awareness of career awareness tools.

MATERIALS: An encyclopedia, old magazines, glue, and scissors.

PROCEDURE:
1. Do the word search and find the nickname of the state.

2. Find the rivers and cities listed in the search. Put them on the blank map on the following page.

3. Make a legend for the minerals and products listed for Michigan. Put them on the same map.

4. President Ford and Henry Ford, the automobile inventor, are from Michigan. Research their life stories. How are they alike? How are they different? Make a time line of Henry Ford's life. Name five ways he has affected your life.

5. Examine some ways the car has helped you have a better life. From old magazines, cut pictures that are related to the car or to the car industry. Make a collage on a piece of paper that has the shape of Michigan.

6. See if you can find some pictures of old cars. Cut them out and make a mobile to hang in your room.

7. What kinds of training would you need to work in an automobile plant? Write a brochure expounding the benefits of working in the state of Michigan.

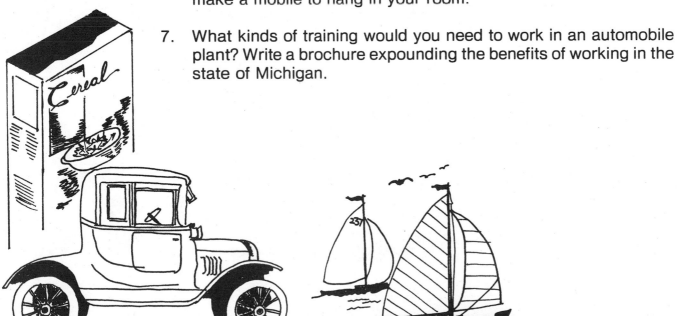

MICHIGAN

MINNESOTA

M	L	O	O	N									
I	T	A	S	C	A	E							
N	T	A	D	N	O	N	O	M	M	O	C		
N	I	O	C	Y	L	I	M	E	S	T	O	N	E
E	R	P	A	O	D	P	O	T	A	T	O	E	S	T	C	A	C	H	S
A	P	M	E	R	N	D	E	E	S	X	A	L	F	L	T	H	T
P	I	R	O	N	S	I	O	U	X	R	I	T	O	O	I
O	G	F	S	A	N	D	T	A	Y	P	F	U	S	P	R
L	E	W	A	L	L	E	Y	E	P	A	D	E	P
I	O	S	E	A	C	E	H	E	R	R	N	E
S	N	N	P	I	L	C	R	C	O	N	W	N
	I	A	R	R	R	E	L	C	I	A	D	K
	P	E	A	E	K	O	H	M	D	G	U
	P	B	P	I	O	E	Y	G	N	A	L
O	I	Y	P	H	S	A	T	I	S	T	U
	S	O	C	T	W	N	B	I	L	N	T
	S	S	E	R	R	B	P	U	N	I	H
	I	R	O	O	I	L	A	K	E	A	T	O
	S	N	C	H	H	P	E	B	R	S	R	N	R
	S	T	I	L	L	W	A	T	E	R	E	G	I	E
	I	M	A	N	G	A	N	E	S	E	D	L	U	A	P
	M	N	A	Y	N	U	B	R	O	I	R	E	P	U	S

Cities
Minneapolis
Saint Paul (2)
Rochester
Stillwater
Hibbing
Saint Cloud (2)

Rivers and Lakes
Minnesota
Red
Itasca
Lake Superior (2)
Mississippi
Pigeon

Indians
Sauk
Sioux
Chippewa

Famous People
Schoolcraft
Duluth
Hennepin
Pike
Mayo
Rice
Ford
Paul Bunyan (2)
Babe (his ox)

Products
Perch
Corn
Flaxseed
Walleye
Oat
Soybeans
Potatoes
Rye
Peas
Barley

Minerals
Iron Ore (2)
Taconite
Granite
Limestone
Manganese
Sand

State Symbols
Bird: Common Loon (2)
Flower: Lady Slipper (2)
Tree: Norway Pine (2)

Put the unused letters all in a row,
And the state nicknames you will know.

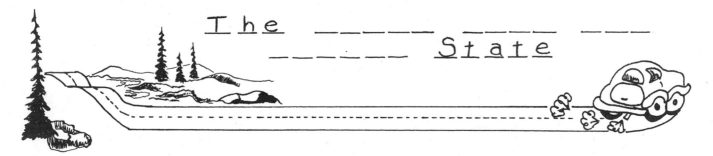

The _ _ _ _ _ _ _ _ _ _ _ _ _ _ _ State

23

MINNESOTA

OBJECTIVES: To improve knowledge of geographical facts about Minnesota.

To improve research skills.

To expand knowledge of natural phenomena of Minnesota.

To encourage awareness of cultural contributions of Minnesota.

MATERIALS: An encyclopedia, drawing paper, crayons, and clay.

PROCEDURE: 1.   Do the word search and find the state's nickname.

2.   On the blank map on the following page, put in the cities and rivers listed in the word search.

3.   Find four more cities and add them to the ones you already have.

4.   Make a legend for the minerals and the products. Add these to your map.

5.   This is known as the "Land of Ten Thousand Lakes." Put in ten of the largest ones. Lake Mille Lacs and Father Hennepin have an interesting story. Research it and share it with your class.

6.   A lumberjack is one who helps cut trees. Paul Bunyan and his ox are part of our natural heritage. Make a model of them out of clay. Look up two or three stories about them. Write one or two to share with your class. What kind of stories are these? How do you suppose they got started?

7.   Minnesota's iron mines are very different from most iron mines. Please analyze the differences. How does it affect the country-side? Is it good or bad? Give five reasons for your opinion.

8.   Rochester has the Mayo Clinic. This is known world-wide for its excellent medical care. Make a time line for this family. How do you think the Mayo Clinic affects the community around it?

MINNESOTA

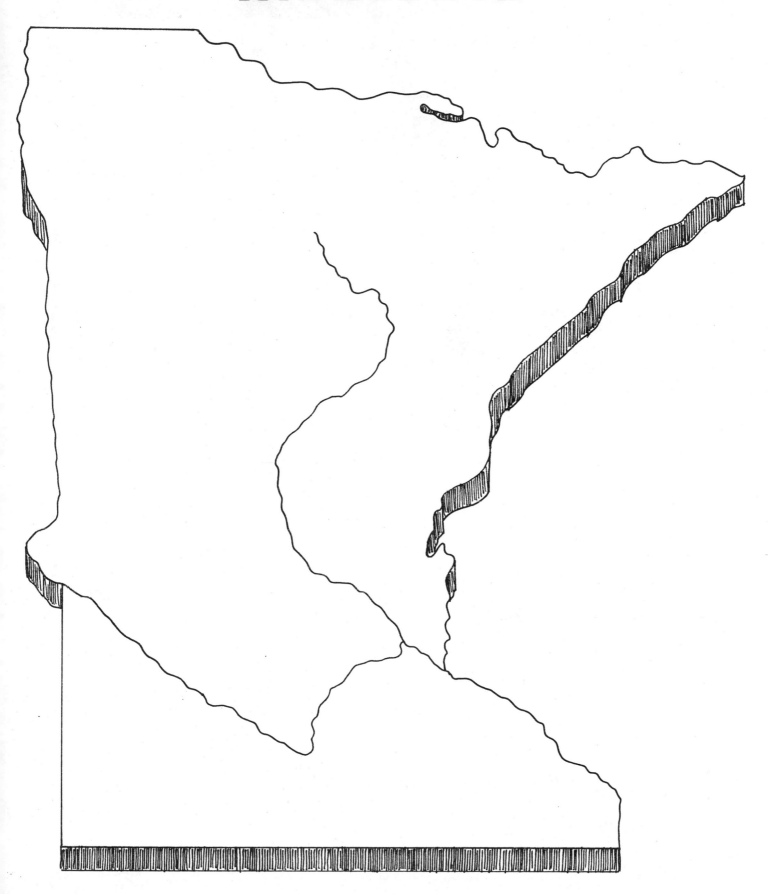

MISSISSIPPI

Cities
Jackson
Natchez
Vicksburg
Hattiesburg
D'Lo
Hub
Arm
Bobo
Meridian

Products
Cotton
Shrimp
Horses
Yam
Fruit
Hogs
Pecans
Beef
Oats

Minerals
Petroleum
Gas
Sand
Bentonite

State Symbols
Bird: Mockingbird
Flower: Magnolia
Tree: Magnolia Tree (2)

Rivers and Lakes
Mississippi
Pearl
Coldwater
Pascagoula
Eagle
Big Black (2)

Indians
Choctaw
Chickasaw
Yazoo
Biloxi

Famous People
Burr
Davis
Turner
Williams
Cavelier

									A
	N	A	T	C	H	E	Z	I	H
C	R	E	N	R	U	T	L	P	A
O	D	N	A	S	B	O	F	P	T
M	L	B	A	A	A	N	R	A	I	T
N	I	D	L	Y	V	G	U	I	W	S	I
A	X	W	A	A	A	I	L	A	S	S	E
I	O	A	C	M	T	O	S	M	R	I	S
D	L	T	K	G	N	A	A	E	E	S	B
I	I	E	N	G	K	I	I	T	A	S	U
R	B	R	A	C	L	L	I	P	G	I	R
E	V	M	I	L	E	N	O	M	L	M	G
M	I	H	I	V	O	L	I	I	E	O	O
A	C	W	A	T	B	U	R	R	P	C	L
S	K	C	N	T	S	G	O	H	E	K	D
A	S	E	H	O	R	S	E	S	T	I	N
G	I	B	O	B	O	O	Z	A	Y	R	N	O
A	L	U	O	G	A	C	S	A	P	O	G	S
P	E	A	R	L	N	O	T	T	O	C	L	B	K
A	R	M	G	B	E	E	F	R	A	T	E	I	C
				E	T	W	U	R	A
				E	S	E	M	D	J
				P	E	C	A	N	S

Put the unused letters on the blanks below.
Then, the state nickname you will know.

The ___ ___ ___ ___ ___ ___ ___   ___ ___ ___ ___ ___

24

MISSISSIPPI

OBJECTIVES: To improve geographical knowledge of the state of Mississippi.

To improve research skills.

To encourage interest in Mississippi's history.

MATERIALS: An encyclopedia, shoe box, old newspaper, pipe cleaners, Popsicle sticks, glue, and a large map of North America.

PROCEDURE:

1. Do the word search and find the state nickname.

2. Put in the cities and rivers listed in the word search and add two more rivers and four more cities on the map on the following page.

3. Make a legend of the minerals and products and add these to your map.

4. Mississippi has "Oxbow" lakes. Find out what these are and why they're peculiar to Mississippi. It also has bayous. What are these? What kinds of plants and animals live there? Write a report on the plant or animal that you think is most interesting.

5. De Soto was an important explorer. On a large map of North America draw his journey. Summarize his life story and his journeys.

6. France sent over young girls to Mississippi in 1721. They were called Casquette girls. Make up a skit to perform with a few friends telling what might have happened to one of these girls.

7. Vicksburg was important in the Civil War. Find out how and why and make a diorama that explains this.

8. Cottonseed oil was first made here. Pretend you're a reporter and publish the story. Interview one of the owners of the plant. Don't forget how, when, where, what, and why questions.

MISSISSIPPI

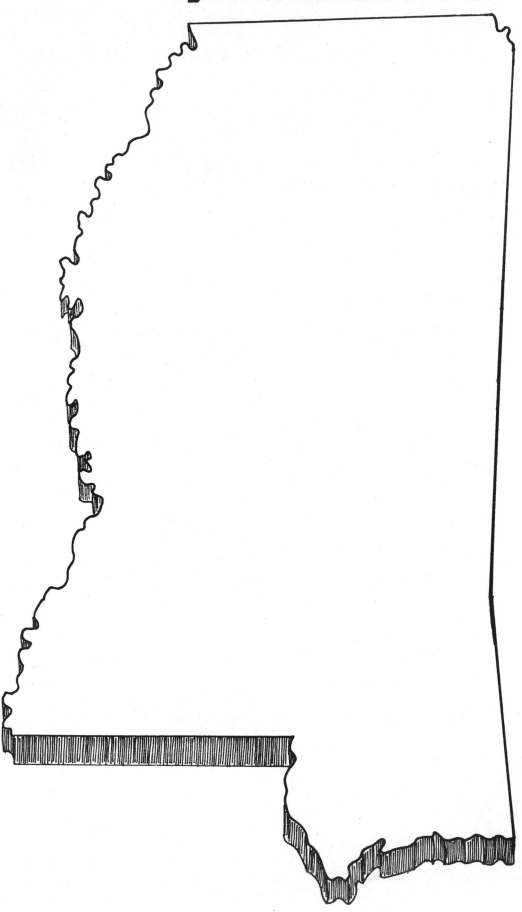

MISSOURI

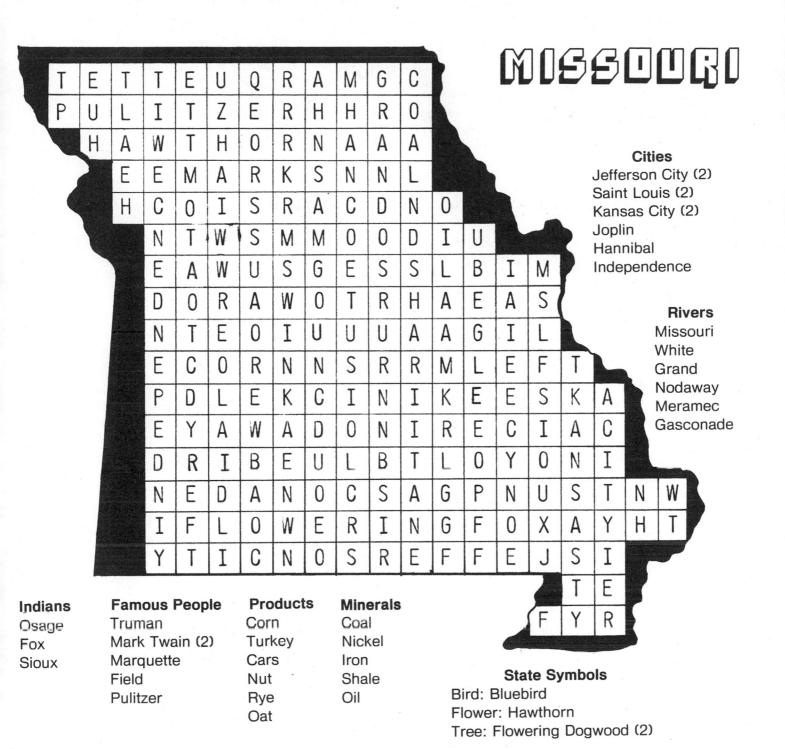

T	E	T	T	E	U	Q	R	A	M	G	C
P	U	L	I	T	Z	E	R	H	H	R	O
H	A	W	T	H	O	R	N	A	A	A	
E	E	M	A	R	K	S	N	N	L		
H	C	O	I	S	R	A	C	D	N	O	
N	T	W	S	M	M	O	O	D	I	U	
E	A	W	U	S	G	E	S	S	L	B	I	M
D	O	R	A	W	O	T	R	H	A	E	A	S
N	T	E	O	I	U	U	U	A	A	G	I	L
E	C	O	R	N	N	S	R	R	M	L	E	F	T
P	D	L	E	K	C	I	N	I	K	E	E	S	K	A
E	Y	A	W	A	D	O	N	I	R	E	C	I	A	C
D	R	I	B	E	U	L	B	T	L	O	Y	O	N	I
N	E	D	A	N	O	C	S	A	G	P	N	U	S	T	N	W
I	F	L	O	W	E	R	I	N	G	F	O	X	A	Y	H	T
Y	T	I	C	N	O	S	R	E	F	F	E	J	S	I
														T	E
													F	Y	R

Cities
Jefferson City (2)
Saint Louis (2)
Kansas City (2)
Joplin
Hannibal
Independence

Rivers
Missouri
White
Grand
Nodaway
Meramec
Gasconade

Indians
Osage
Fox
Sioux

Famous People
Truman
Mark Twain (2)
Marquette
Field
Pulitzer

Products
Corn
Turkey
Cars
Nut
Rye
Oat

Minerals
Coal
Nickel
Iron
Shale
Oil

State Symbols
Bird: Bluebird
Flower: Hawthorn
Tree: Flowering Dogwood (2)

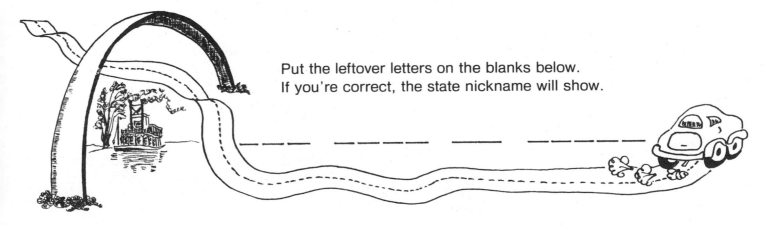

Put the leftover letters on the blanks below.
If you're correct, the state nickname will show.

25

MISSOURI

OBJECTIVES: To improve geographical knowledge of Missouri.

To encourage research skills.

To promote use of career awareness tools.

MATERIALS: An encyclopedia, salt, flour, water, cardboard, watercolors, blue yarn, and a large map of the United States.

PROCEDURE:

1. Do the word search and find the nickname of the state.

2. Put in the listed cities and rivers on the map on the following page. Please include the Mississippi River as well as four more. Then put in six more cities.

3. Make a legend for the minerals and the products listed. Put these on the map that follows.

4. Find the area the Indians lived in. Color each region a distinctive color. Make a legend and include these on your map.

5. Put each famous person's birthplace in, beside his name.

6. On a large map of the United States trace the Oregon Trail and the Santa Fe Trail. Tell why they were important to Missouri's economy.

7. Make a gameboard for you and a friend to play. Use the theme of capturing Jesse James and his gang. Start at the bank that was robbed: strong horses were tied near the bank, go ahead two spaces; your horse threw a shoe, lose a turn; an Indian saw the gang, get an extra turn; a bad rainstorm, lose a turn; a mountaineer gives you wrong directions, go back three spaces; you see their smoke from their campfire, get an extra turn; you catch the gang but they hid the money, lose a turn; you find the money in a cave, you win and collect the reward.

8. Trace the shape of the state. Copy it on cardboard. Using a mixture of two parts of flour to one part of salt, moisten enough to be pliable. Make the state with its mountains on the cardboard. Use the blue yarn for rivers. Paint it when dry and add the cities and rivers.

MISSOURI

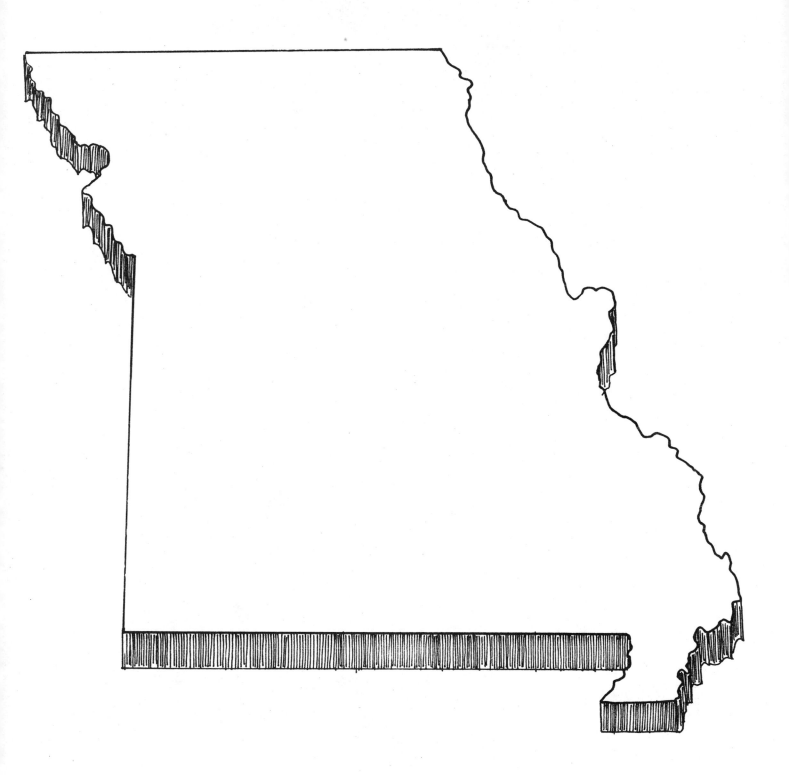

MONTANA

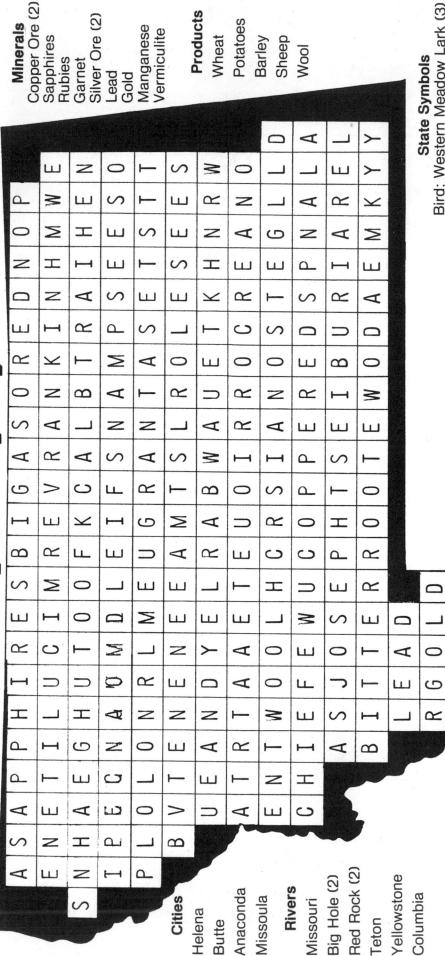

Minerals
Copper Ore (2)
Sapphires
Rubies
Garnet
Silver Ore (2)
Lead
Gold
Manganese
Vermiculite

Products
Wheat
Potatoes
Barley
Sheep
Wool

State Symbols
Bird: Western Meadow Lark (3)
Flower: Bitterroot
Tree: Ponderosa Pine (2)

Cities
Helena
Butte
Anaconda
Missoula

Rivers
Missouri
Big Hole (2)
Red Rock (2)
Teton
Yellowstone
Columbia

Famous People
Custer
Chief Joseph (2)
Grant
Plummer
Daly
Mansfield
Wheeler
Rankin

Indians
Arapaho
Atsina
Blackfoot
Cheyenne
Crow

Put the unused letters on the blanks below.
If you are right, the state nickname will show.

The __ __ __ __ __ __ __ __ __ __ __

26

MONTANA

OBJECTIVES: To improve the geographical knowledge of Montana.

To encourage research skills.

To promote understanding of natural phenomena of Montana.

MATERIALS: An encyclopedia, shoe box, long strips of plain paper, two old pencils, crayons, glue, and scissors.

PROCEDURE:

1. Do the word search and find the state nickname.

2. Put in the cities and rivers listed on the blank map on the following page. Add five cities and three rivers of your own choosing.

3. Make a legend for the products and minerals. Put these in place on the map.

4. Find where the Indians and famous people lived. Color the five Indian territories. Place the names of the famous people wherever they influenced the state.

5. Montana has a park with a glacier. Research glaciers. Make a report as to how and why they occur. Tell how they influence the territory around them. Do they move? How fast? Are they safe to walk on? Why or why not?

6. Make a brochure encouraging people to come visit Montana. Display its attractions.

7. Using a shoe box and the long strips of paper make a little car to use in the front of the box. Make a background that you can move on pencils to show what kinds of scenery you would see if you drove across Montana.

8. *Custer's Last Stand* is a famous painting. Find out about the battle. What started it? Where did it take place? Who were the people involved? On a large piece of paper make your own drawing of the battle.

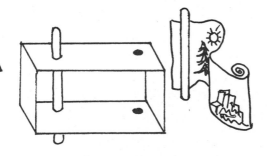

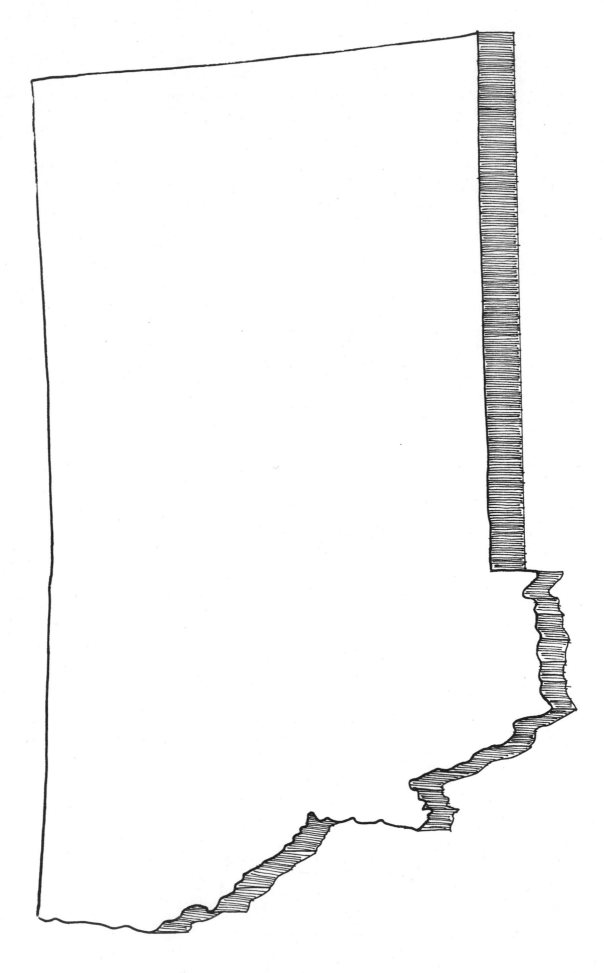

MONTANA

NEBRASKA

C	O	R	O	N	A	D	O	G	A	B	E	N	N	I	W				
A	R	A	R	B	O	I	N	C	U	E	T	T	A	L	P	I	L	E	L
V	M	U	H	G	R	O	S	F	C	H	W	E	S	R	O	H	R	I	E	A	O
E	G	R	A	N	D	K	F	O	T	O	R	G	N	S	A	N	D	U	N	N	R
L	L	I	B	P	N	A	R	O	D	G	N	N	Y	Z	A	R	C	A	O	C	W	K
I	O	W	A	U	L	N	Y	A	X	I	R	D	H	M	U	E	K	I	P	S	O	A
E	L	K	F	O	R	K	E	T	T	E	U	S	E	L	A	S	A	L	L	E	S	L	P
R	A	M	A	L	I	M	E	S	T	O	N	E	O	H	A	P	A	R	A	K	E	I	N
		G	A	S	L	R	R	E	D	R	P	E	T	R	O	L	E	U	M
		H	E	C	F	F	U	L	B	S	T	T	O	C	S	F	E	E	B
	W	H	E	A	T	J	E	F	F	E	R	S	O	N	R	U	O	L	F
	G	O	L	D	E	N	R	O	D	D	O	O	W	N	O	T	T	O	C

Cities
Scottsbluff
Nebraska (City)
Grand Fork (2)
Hastings
Lincoln
Lamar
Funk
Elk (City)

Rivers
Platte
Missouri
Loup
Niobrára

State Symbols
Bird: Western Meadow Lark (3)
Flower: Goldenrod
Tree: Cottonwood

Indians
Fox
Iowa
Winnebago
Arapaho
Oto
Pawnee

Famous People
Freeman
Cavelier
La Sale
Buffalo Bill (2)
Coronado
Crazy Horse (2)
Red Cloud (2)
Jefferson
Pike

Products
Beef
Corn
Wheat
Sorghum
Oats
Flour
Hog
Rye

Minerals
Gas
Petroleum
Limestone
Sand

Put the unused letters all in row.
If you're right, the state nickname will show.

The _____
_____ State

79

27

NEBRASKA

OBJECTIVES: To promote geographical knowledge of the state of Nebraska.

To improve research skills.

To encourage political knowledge of the state of Nebraska.

MATERIALS: An encyclopedia, clay, Popsicle sticks, and an old handkerchief.

PROCEDURE:
1. Do the word search and find the state nickname.

2. Put in the cities and rivers listed on the state map that follows. Add five more cities and three more rivers to make your map more interesting.

3. Make a legend for the minerals and products of the state. Add these to your map.

4. Make a legend for the territories of the Indian tribes. Color these on your map.

5. Put in either the birthplace or the place where the famous people listed had the most influence. Add this to your map, too.

6. On a map you have traced from the one in the book, label the Mormon Trail and the Oregon Trail on this map.

7. Make a model of a Conestoga wagon from the Popsicle sticks, handkerchief, and clay.

8. Nebraska has the only state legislature that just has one legislative body. Explain how it works. Why did they decide on just one body? What do you think are the advantages or disadvantages of it? On a large sheet of paper, diagram the process a bill would follow if you were to submit it to the group for consideration.

9. Most people who homesteaded in Nebraska lived in sod houses. Make a model out of clay. Name three advantages and three disadvantages of sod houses.

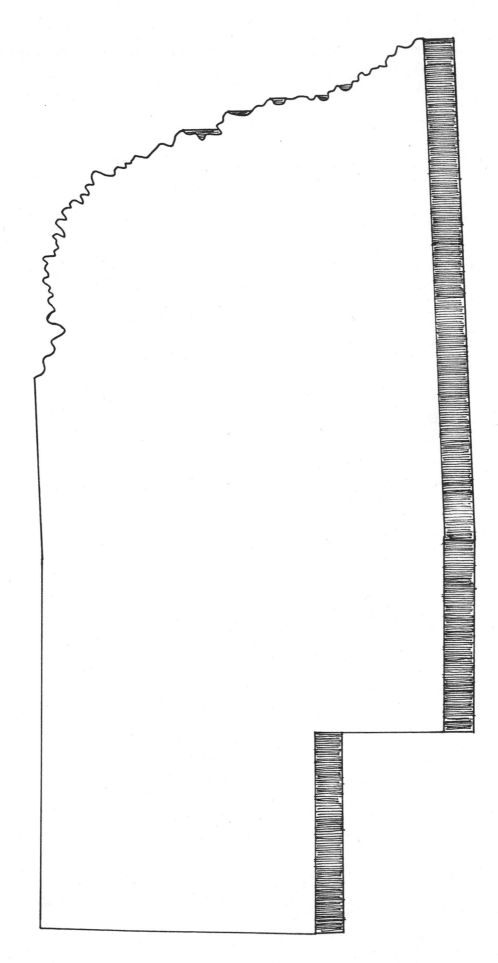

NEBRASKA

Nevada

Cities
Carson City (2)
Henderson
Reno
Tonopah
Mina
Elko
Virginia (City)
Las Vegas (2)
Ely

Rivers
Humboldt
Colorado
Reese
Walker
Truckee

Products
Cotton
Beef
Sheep
Hen
Figs
Wool
Oat
Hay

Famous People
Smith
Frémont
Wovoka
Pittman
Wolfskill

Minerals
Magnesium
Copper
Titanium
Tungsten
Gypsum
Gold
Mercury
Lead
Lime

Indians
Mohave
Paiute
Washoe
Basket Maker (2)
Pueblo
Shoshoni

State Symbols
Bird: Mountain Bluebird (2)
Flower: Sagebrush
Tree: Single-Leaf Piñon (3)

S	Y	R	U	C	R	E	M	U	I	N	A	T	I	T
A	A	Y	L	E	P	U	E	B	L	O	W	O	O	L
G	B	G	E	S	S	A	L	M	I	N	A	N	C	L
E	E	S	E	P	A	I	U	T	E	I	O	P	A	I
B	E	I	Y	V	I	I	E	C	O	P	P	E	R	K
R	F	G	L	R	S	T	O	V	A	V	H	E	S	S
U	C	Y	T	E	E	L	T	H	A	E	E	H	O	F
S	A	O	N	R	O	K	T	M	N	H	H	S	N	L
H	H	G	T	R	U	I	A	D	A	U	O	V	R	O
S	A	O	A	T	M	C	E	M	M	N	I	M	F	W
M	I	D	S	S	O	R	K	B	T	R	S	R	R	T
	O	N	E	H	S	N	O	E	G	E	E	E	U	A
	U	G	O	O	L	G	I	E	M	K	N	L	D
	N	L	D	N	N	M	O	L	G	S	E	R
	T	E	I	I	N	A	S	E	O	A	I
	A	L	T	W	T	B	H	Y	D	B
	I	E	E	O	S	D	T	O	E
	N	A	A	V	L	I	N	U
	W	F	S	O	C	E	L
	R	E	G	K	R	B
	U	L	I	A	F
	S	K	F
	H	O

Please put the leftover letters all in a row.
If you are right, the state nicknames will show.

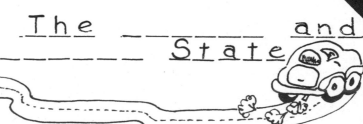

The _ _ _ _ _ _ _ and
_ _ _ _ _ _ _ _ _ _ State

28

NEVADA

OBJECTIVES: To improve geographical knowledge of the state of Nevada.

To encourage research skills.

To arouse interest in natural phenomena of Nevada.

MATERIALS: An encyclopedia, cardboard, watercolors, old magazines, glue, and scissors.

PROCEDURE: 1.   Do the word search and find the nickname of the state.

2.   Put in the listed cities and rivers and add a few of your own choice on the blank map which follows this page.

3.   Make a legend for the minerals and products listed. Put these in where they are found or manufactured. Add five more minerals and three products that you think are interesting.

4.   Research where the Indians and famous people lived. Color in the areas for the Indians.

5.   Nevada has the least amount of rainfall of any state in the Union. Find out how that affects what agriculture they have. How do they compensate? Only a few of the rivers empty into the sea. Where do the rest go? Prepare a report for your class on Nevada's rivers.

6.   Las Vegas is the gambling capital of the state. It attracts many visitors every year. What else do you think there is to entertain people? Make a big poster advertising Las Vegas and the other attractions in this state.

7.   Find out about R. C. Gridley and his sack of flour. It was auctioned off over and over. Why? What was this the forerunner of? Pretend you were there. How do you think he achieved this? Prepare a collage on a paper sack of flour from old magazines using pictures of the things the money would provide for the needy.

Nevada

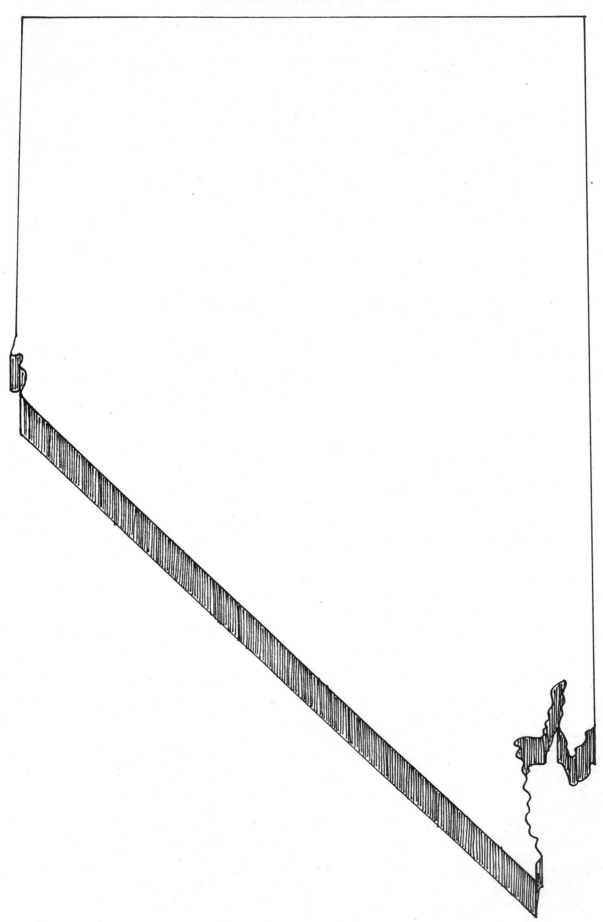

NEW HAMPSHIRE

Cities
Concord
Manchester
Rochester
Nashua

Indians
Pennacook
Squamscot
Piscataqua
Iroquois

Products
Leather
Fruit
Clam
Cod
Lobsters
Rye

Rivers
Connecticut
Merrimack
Ellis
Baker

Famous People
Pierce
Shepard
Dearborn
Champlain

Minerals
Mica Ore (2)
Feldspar

State Symbols
Bird: (Purple) Finch
Flower: (Purple) Lilac
Tree: (White) Birch

```
                        E  T
                     H  L  C
                  H  P  L  O
                  C  I  I  N
                  R  S  S  N
            E  I  C  N  E
            G  B  A  I  C
            R  S  T  A  T
            H  A  A  L  I  C
      U  C  N  Q  P  C
   A  A  M  S  U  M  U
   L  L  F  H  A  A  A  T
R  I  E  E  I  N  L  H  I
L  A  P  A  C  N  T  C  T
P  A  P  H  T  R  C  O  D
I  R  E  E  S  E  H  C  H  D
D  D  R  S  N  T  D  S  E  E  R
E  B  T  O  S  N  M  L  C  R  O
A  E  A  E  Q  A  A  R  E  F  C  A
R  E  H  K  U  U  E  C  R  F  N  C
B  C  E  Q  E  I  O  U  O  S  O  I  T
E  O  Y  S  A  P  R  I  I  T  O  C  M
R  R  L  O  B  S  T  E  R  S  E  K
O  N  K  C  A  M  I  R  R  E  M
```

Put the unused letters in a row as you go.
If you're correct, the state nickname will show.

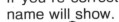

_____ _____ _____ _____ _____ _____ _____ _____ _____ _____ _____ _____ _____ _____

85

29

NEW HAMPSHIRE

OBJECTIVES: To enrich geographical knowledge of the state of New Hampshire.

To encourage research skills.

To arouse interest in New Hampshire's history.

MATERIALS: An encyclopedia and clay.

PROCEDURE:
1. Do the word search and find the state nickname.

2. Please put in the named cities and draw in the rivers listed. Use the blank map on the following page.

3. Add three rivers of your own choosing and five more cities.

4. Please make a legend for the minerals and products listed. Put these in on the map along with the cities and rivers.

5. Daniel Webster was one of the great statesmen of the revolutionary period. Make a time line of his life story.

6. Concord coaches were much in demand. Make a model out of clay.

7. Alan Shepard was the first American to travel in space. Pretend you were a reporter at his lift-off. Write a story for your paper. Don't forget the questions: how, when, where, why, and who.

8. New Hampshire leads in leather manufacturing. Shoes are its most important product. On a large sheet of paper, draw the steps in putting a shoe together.

NEW HAMPSHIRE

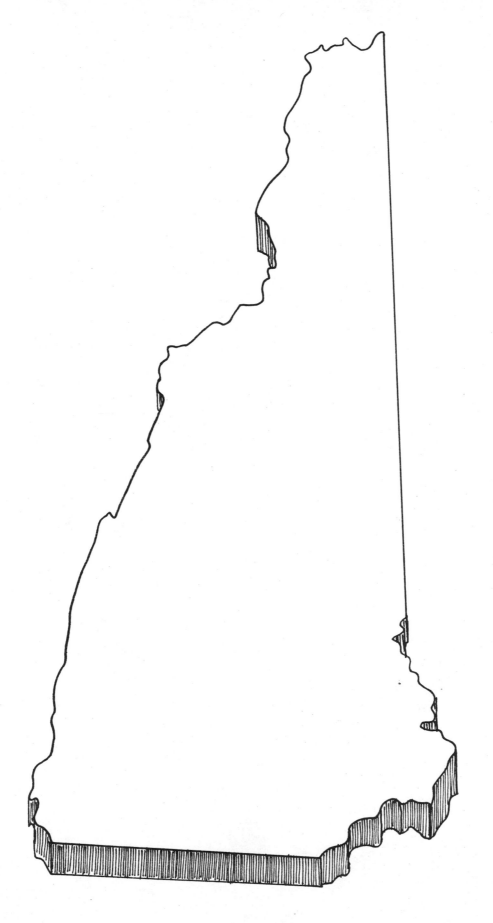

NEW JERSEY

Cities
Trenton
Princeton
Newark
Morristown
Perth Amboy (2)

Rivers
Raritan
Tom's
Musconetcong
Hudson

Indians
Algonkian
Delaware

Products
Beef
Squash
Corn
Cars
Yams
Wine
Hay

Minerals
Zinc
Sand
Stone
Titanium Ore (2)
Iron

Famous People
Edison
Einstein
Morse
Mey
Hart
Case
Wilson

State Symbols
Bird: (Eastern) Goldfinch
Flower: (Purple) Violet
Tree: Red Oak (2)

						T						
					G	H	R	S				
				M	N	N	T	E	R			
				O	O	P	O	R	N	A	T	
			M	R	C	R	A	S	E	T	C	H
			U	R	T	I	M	E	L	P	O	V
			I	I	E	N	B	C	G	I	I	N
		Y	N	S	N	C	O	A	O	O	W	
		A	A	T	O	E	Y	S	L	G		
		M	T	O	C	T	A	E	D	R		
		S	I	W	S	O	T	N	F	U		
			T	N	U	N	A	E	I	D	H	
					M	S	E	N	N	N	Y	
						O	A	O	C	A	Z	
					N	I	R	T	H	I	S	
				O	K	N	N	S	N	F		
			S	N	C	A	O	C	E	E		
	T	I	O	Q	T	O	N	R	R	E		
A	D	G	H	I	U	E	R	A	I	B		
E	L	W	R	A	W	A	W	N	T			
A	M	A	I	A	R	A	S	E				
O	R	E	R	N	L	T	T	H				
	A	K	Y	E	E	O						
		K	D	I	M	R						
			N	S	E							
				D								

Please put the unused letters on the blanks below.
If you're correct, the state nickname will show.

___ ___ ___

___ ___ ___ ___ ___ ___ ___ ___ ___

___ ___ ___ ___ ___ ___

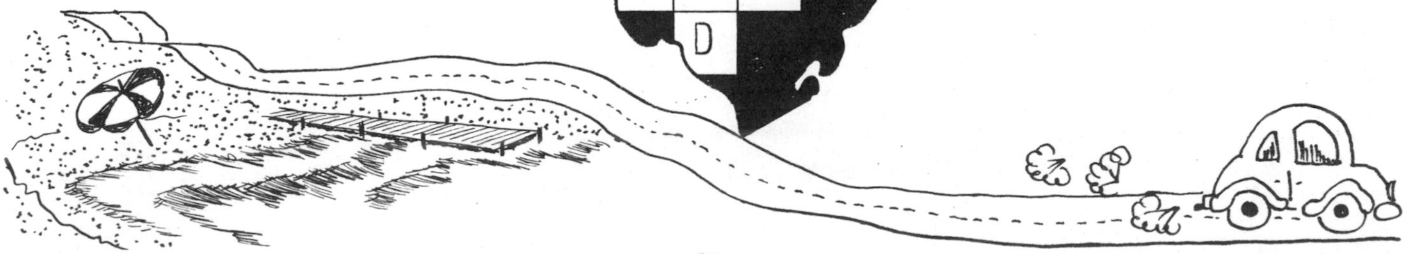

30

NEW JERSEY

OBJECTIVES: To promote geographical knowledge of New Jersey.

To improve research skills.

To encourage use of career awareness tools.

MATERIALS: An encyclopedia.

PROCEDURE: 1.   Do the word search and find the state nickname.

2.   On the following page is a blank map of the state. Please put in the listed cities and draw in the rivers that are named.

3.   On the same map, add five cities and three rivers of your own choice.

4.   Please show the products and minerals on the state map, after you make a legend for them.

5.   Molly Pitcher was a famous lady of the Revolutionary War. Draw a large picture showing her brave deed. Under it, in a few sentences, tell her story.

6.   New Jersey is the place where three of the most important inventions were perfected. Choose one and prepare a skit with a friend telling what you think happened. Present it to your class.

7.   If you were interested in a career in one of these fields, what kind of a scholastic background would you need? Make a diagram listing other related fields you might choose.

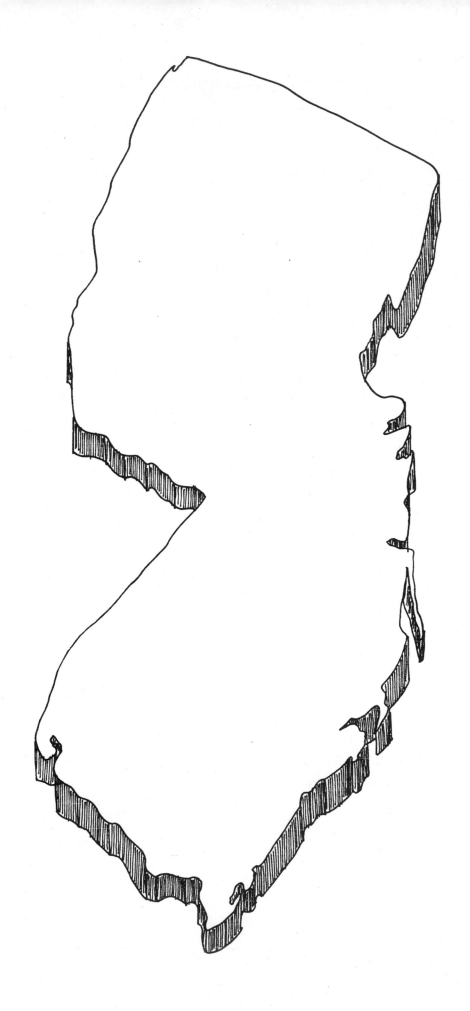

NEW JERSEY

NEW MEXICO

```
C H I L L S R E N N U R D A O R
A P E T I R O N O T G N I M R A F
N O L L O G O M H S S A N T A F E
A H I A E Y A G E W R H D L O G R
D G U O N E C A E C L E A D I L
I I M C A R U A V L N H D E O O E
A L C S O R A L F H L S A G P S U
N A N C P I N O N S U R C S N Q
E Z I S N P C I O C A P S O A R
I M A H T N L E R U N O T S C C E
O L U A O L A D R D M U R O E E U
D V O H E H A U E A N N P P Q
A G I W G B A T J A C I T M E T U
N T S L S R I V E N N M I F E E B
O O I L H O P A U J K O C O L
R D R E W A N S Z N O S R E D N A
O A P A C H E
C V T
```

Cities
Santa Fe
Albuquerque
Gallup
Vado
Roswell
Las Cruces
Carlsbad
Farmington
Loco Hills (2)

Rivers
Canadian
Gila
Pecos
Rio Grande
San Juan
Chaco
Ute (Creek)

Famous People
Anderson
Coronado
Geronimo
Kit Carson (2)
Ross
Lew
Villa
Jim White (2)

Indians
Apache
Hopi
Navaho
Zuñi
Mogollon
Anasazi

Minerals
Iron
Silver
Gold
Lead
Potash
Coal
Uranium
Copper
Helium
Oil
Gas

Products
Sheep
Pecans
Goats
Corn
Sorghum
Peanuts
Beef

State Symbols
Bird: Roadrunner
Flower: Yucca (Flower)
Tree: Piñon

Put the unused letters on the blanks below.
If you are right, the state nickname will show.

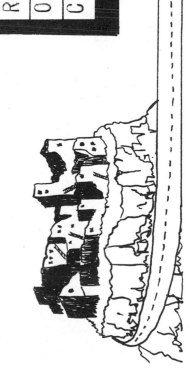

31

NEW MEXICO

OBJECTIVES: To encourage geographical knowledge of New Mexico.

To improve research skills.

To promote interest in different Indian cultures that inhabited New Mexico.

MATERIALS: An encyclopedia, two shoe boxes, clay, Popsicle sticks, toothpicks, yarn, scissors, watercolors or crayons, paper sacks, and glue.

PROCEDURE: 1.   Do the word search and find the state nickname.

2.   On the following page is a blank map of the state. Please put in place the cities listed. Then draw in the rivers.

3.   Make a legend for the minerals and the products named. Put these on your map.

4.   Research where the Indian tribes lived. Color in each territory to show the range of the Indians' wanderings.

5.   Make two dioramas depicting the life-style of the Mogollon Indians and the Anasazi tribes. How were they different? How were they alike? You will need the shoe boxes, clay, Popsicle sticks, toothpicks, yarn, glue, colors, and scissors.

6.   Use the paper sacks to depict their gods. Contrast the "faith" of these two tribes. Make a puppet to show the god of each.

7.   Carlsbad Caverns were first explored in the early part of this century. What are the kinds of minerals found there? What causes the strange formations in a cave of this size? What are the pillars called? What are the names of the icicle-shaped rocks that form on the ceilings of caves? What are the men called who explore caves? What kinds of training do you think they need?

NEW MEXICO

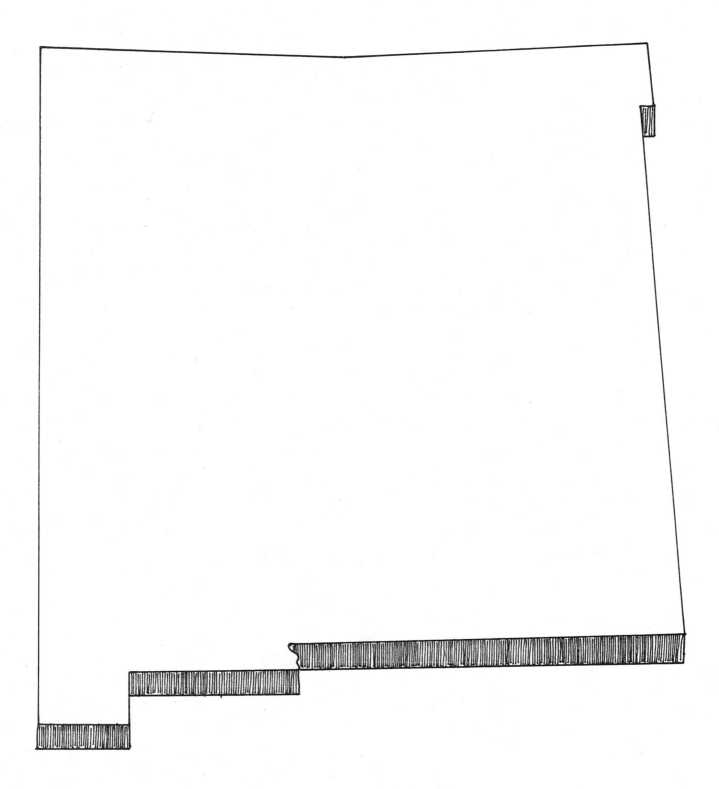

NEW YORK

Rivers
Delaware Hudson
Beaver   Niagara
Saint Lawrence

Indians
Algonkian
Iroquois
Oneida

Cities
New York City (3)
Buffalo
Rochester
Yonkers
Rome
Albany
Syracuse
Evans (Mills)
Utica

Famous People
Washington
Roosevelt
Fulton
Fillmore
Van Buren (2)
Mott
(John) Jay

Products
Cheese   Flounder
Grain   Cod
Bees   Beef
Hay   Wine

Minerals
Zinc Ore (2)
Gas
Stone
Clay

State Symbols
Bird: Bluebird
Flower: Rose
Tree: Sugar Maple (2)

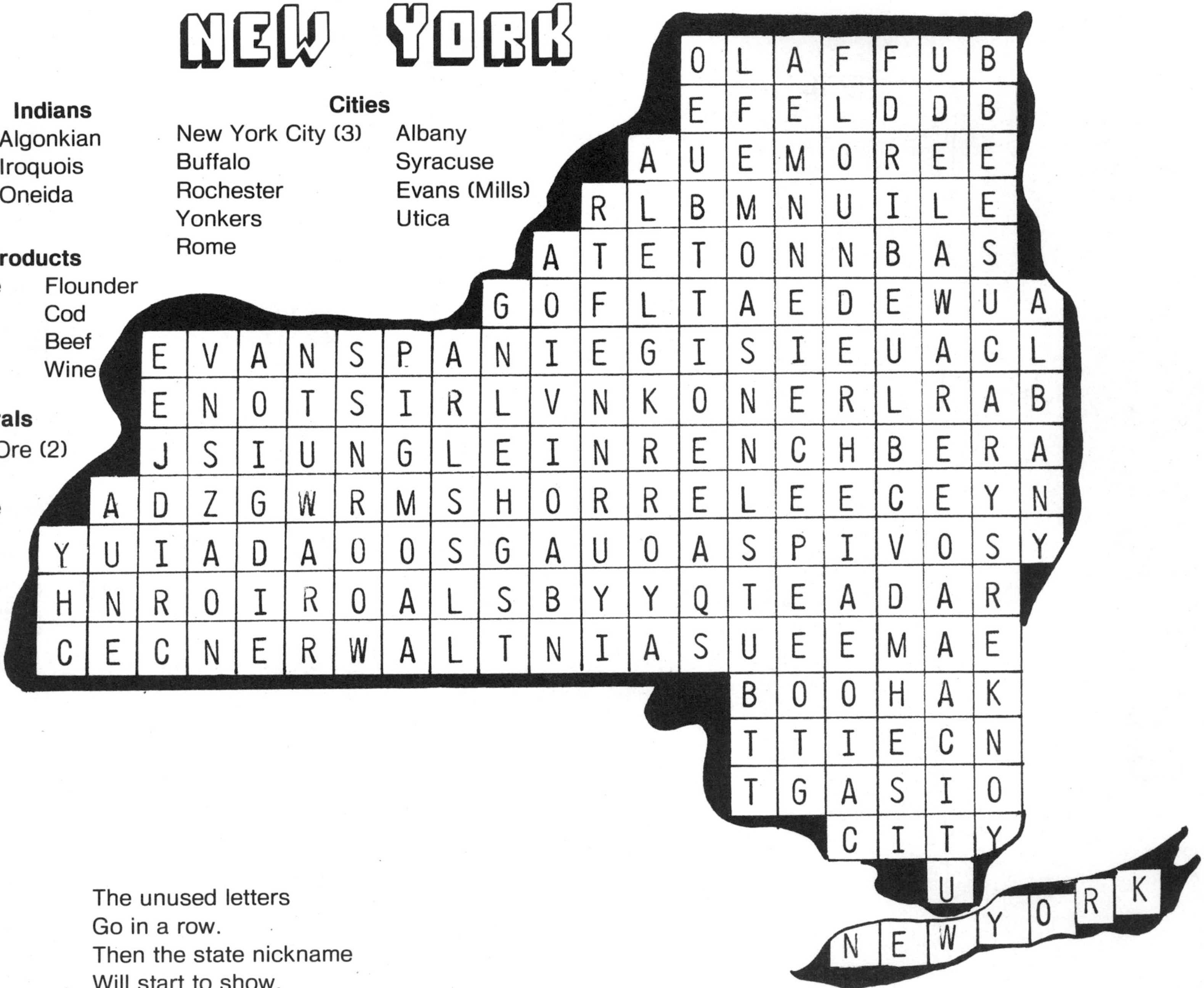

```
O L A F F U B
E F E L D D B
A U E M O R E E        A
  R L B M N U I L E     W U
  A T E T O N N B A S   E D E
G O F L T A E D W U A   A C L
A N E G I S I E U A C L R A B
N T S I R L V N K O N E R L R A B
J S I U N G L E I N R E N C H B E R A
A D Z G W R M S H O R R E L E E C E Y N
Y I A D A O O S G A U O A S P I V O S Y
H N R O I R O A L S B Y Y Q T E A D A R
C E C N E R W A L T N I A S U E E M A E
              B O O H A K
              T T I E C N
              T G A S I O
                C I T Y U

                    N E W Y O R K
                    N E W Y O R K
```

The unused letters
Go in a row.
Then the state nickname
Will start to show.

The E m p i r e ___ ___ ___ ___ ___

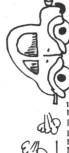

94

32

NEW YORK

OBJECTIVES: To encourage geographical knowledge of New York.

To promote use of research skills.

To cultivate interest in historical knowledge of New York.

To arouse interest in career opportunities found in New York City.

MATERIALS: An encyclopedia, clay, large piece of paper suitable for a mural, watercolors or crayons, and cardboard.

PROCEDURE:

1. Do the word search and find the state nickname.

2. On the following page is a blank map of the state. Put in the cities listed and draw in the rivers named. Add ten more cities and five more rivers.

3. Make a legend for the products and minerals listed. Put them on the blank state.

4. New York has a different shape. See if you can make something else out of it, like an animal head.

5. The Statue of Liberty is in need of repair. Research her story. Find out where she came from and why she is so important.

6. Niagara Falls is considered one of the wonders of the world. Copy a picture of it. How long and how high is it? How many gallons of water go over it in a day? What kind of training would you need to be involved in maintaining it? It is a great source of electricity. What careers would you find useful for this?

7. Make a brochure promoting career opportunities in New York City. Illustrate the advantages of living in this large city.

8. The Erie Canal; Henry Hudson; and the *Clermont*, the first steamboat, were all part of New York's history. On your paper for the mural, illustrate the story of one of these.

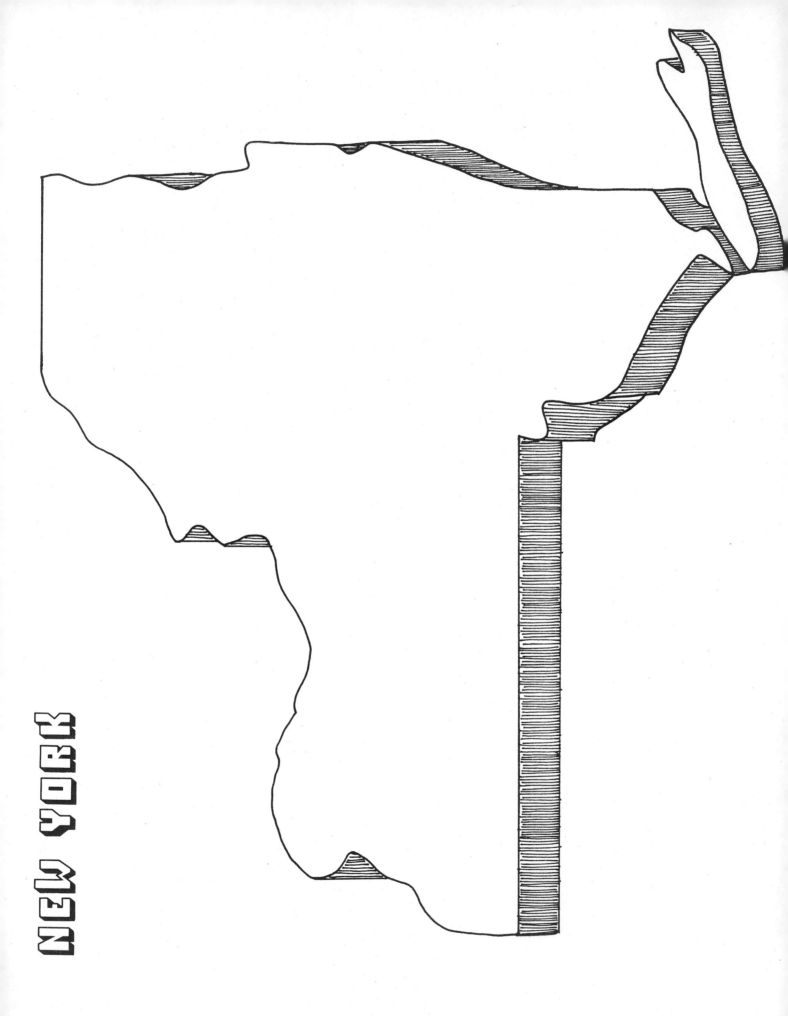

NEW YORK

NORTH CAROLINA

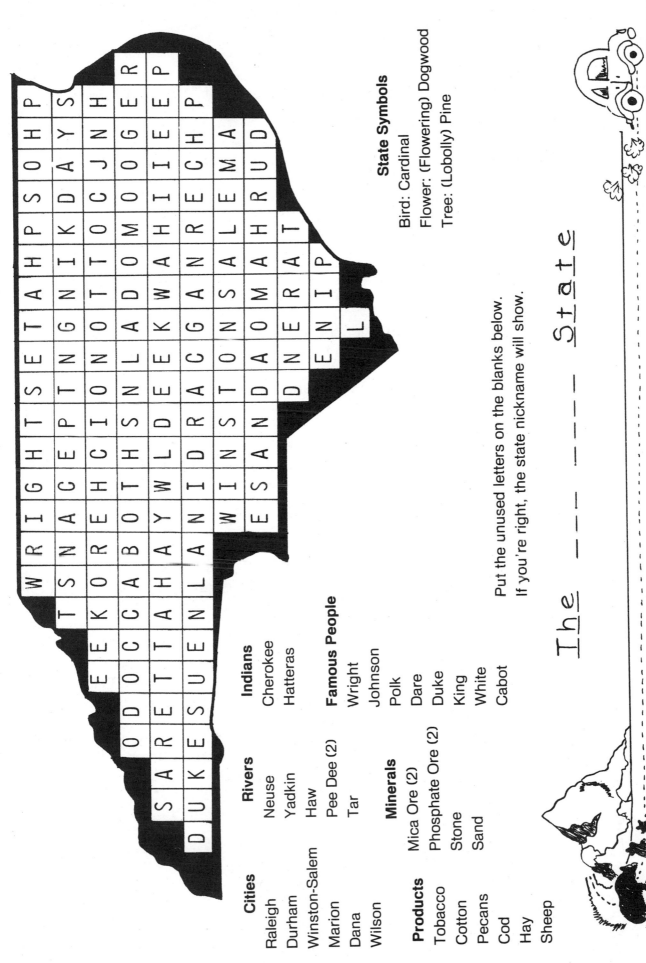

Cities
Raleigh
Durham
Winston-Salem
Marion
Dana
Wilson

Rivers
Neuse
Yadkin
Haw
Pee Dee (2)
Tar

Indians
Cherokee
Hatteras

Famous People
Wright
Johnson
Polk
Dare
Duke
King
White
Cabot

Minerals
Mica Ore (2)
Phosphate Ore (2)
Stone
Sand

Products
Tobacco
Cotton
Pecans
Cod
Hay
Sheep

State Symbols
Bird: Cardinal
Flower: (Flowering) Dogwood
Tree: (Lobolly) Pine

Put the unused letters on the blanks below.
If you're right, the state nickname will show.

The __ __ __ __ __ State

97

33

NORTH CAROLINA

OBJECTIVES: To encourage geographical knowledge of North Carolina.

To improve research skills.

To increase historical knowledge of North Carolina.

MATERIALS: An encyclopedia, paper sacks, yarn, and cardboard.

PROCEDURE:
1. Do the word search and find the nickname.

2. On the following page, there is a blank map of the state. Find the rivers and cities listed in the word search. Put them on the map.

3. Please make a legend for the products and minerals for North Carolina. Add these to the same map as the rivers and cities.

4. Cape Hatteras is very dangerous for ships. Find out why it is called the "Graveyard of the Atlantic." What effect did this have on the state?

5. Blackbeard was one of the most famous and feared pirates. Write his life story. With the paper sack make a puppet of him. Be sure you paint on his famous beard. Use black yarn for his hair. Be sure you make a pirate hat out of black construction paper for the puppet.

6. The Wright brothers flew the first plane at Kitty Hawk. Make a time line of their lives. Make a small plane like theirs as a model to show the class. Use cardboard for the wings.

7. North Carolina is known as the "Tobacco Capital." There are two different kinds grown there. Illustrate each. Tell what they're used for. How are they alike? How are they different? Make a short report to share with your class.

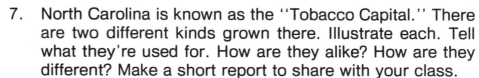

8. In 1587 a colony was established on Roanoke Island. It was known as the "Lost Colony." Pretend you're a reporter. Interview one of the residents. Find out what happened to them and why. Remember the who, how, when, where, and why questions of good reporting.

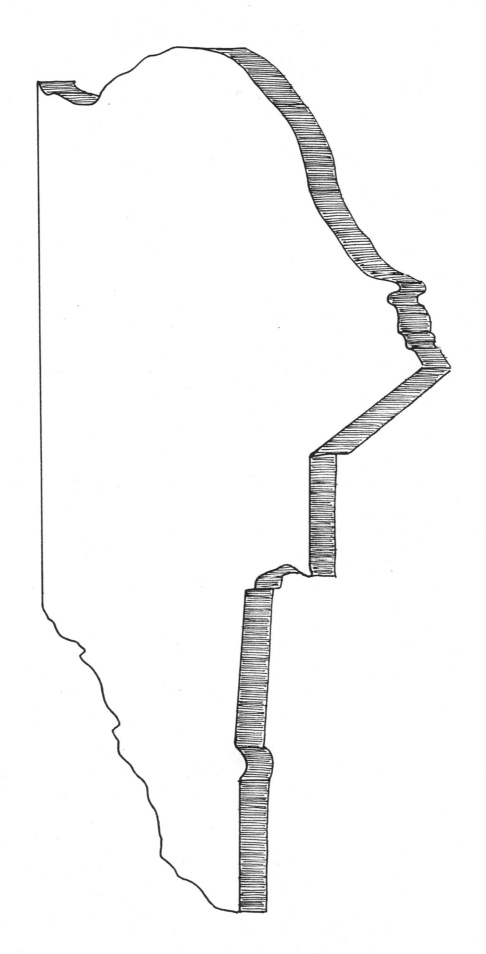

NORTH CAROLINA

NORTH DAKOTA

A	F	G	R	A	N	D	D	L	I	W	I	R	O	U	S	I	M	F	
M	S	A	L	T	E	A	S	T	A	D	I	H	O	S	T	A	O	O	S
E	A	S	R	V	I	P	A	G	E	C	F	L	C	S	A	F	R	T	O
R	N	U	I	G	E	W	O	Y	E	X	L	L	D	G	E	K	A	C	F
I	D	L	R	N	O	M	R	T	O	M	A	T	O	E	S	E	H	O	G	L
C	S	A	N	D	I	D	A	A	Y	X	I	B	S	H	E	E	P	E	I
A	I	K	A	N	N	B	W	N	C	T	T	K	U	W	Y	L	K	N	E	K
N	R	E	O	E	A	O	M	D	E	O	G	H	E	L	M	N	R	C	L
R	M	T	R	R	P	S	U	I	T	A	A	E	N	A	A	E	R	A	T
E	A	E	L	P	I	K	I	I	N	R	N	N	S	P	Y	L	A	O	I	L
T	V	E	I	O	N	K	N	I	F	E	E	A	L	E	T	M	C	D	E	R	C
S	Y	H	U	A	R	G	R	A	V	E	L	E	H	T	S	I	T	I	N	G
E	C	X	R	A	I	L	E	K	R	U	B	S	A	I	E	I	R	I	A	R	P
W	B	U	L	L	A	B	N	O	N	N	A	C	B	I	N	O	H	S	O	H	S

Put the unused letters all in a row. If you're right, the state nickname you'll know.

The ___ ___ and ___ ___ State

Cities
Bismarck
Grand Forks (2)
Minot
Fargo
Devils Lake (2)
Tioga
Penn
Page

Rivers
Knife
Red
Missouri
Cannonball
Sheyenne
Wild Rice (2)
Maple

Minerals
Clay
Lignite
Coal
Oil
Uranium
Gas
Salt
Sand

Indians
Cheyenne
Hidatsa
Assiniboin
Sioux
Shoshoni
Chippewa

Famous People
Mandan
Vérendrye
Clark
La Salle
Sitting Bull (2)
Burke

Products
Barley
Flax
Potatoes
Sheep
Sugar Beet (2)
Grain
Hog
Cattle
Oats
Wheat
Tomatoes
Hay
Gravel

State Symbols
Bird: Western Meadow Lark (3)
Flower: Wild Prairie Rose (3)
Tree: American Elm (2)

NORTH DAKOTA

OBJECTIVES: To promote geographical knowledge of North Dakota.

To improve research skills.

To encourage the use of career awareness tools by the student.

MATERIALS: An encyclopedia, old magazines, scissors, glue, clay, and toothpicks.

PROCEDURE: 1.   Do the word search and find the nickname of North Dakota.

2.   Please put the listed cities and rivers on the blank map on the following page. Then add ten cities and three rivers of your own choice.

3.   Make a legend for the products and minerals found here. Put them on the map.

4.   Make a collage of pictures cut from the old magaines that would advertise or relate to the minerals and products found here. Trace the shape of the state and use that as your background.

5.   Bonanza farms were prominent here. What were they? How did they get their name? When did they flourish? Who started them? Make a chart showing the production of wheat in this state from 1850 until now.

6.   Mandan Indians lived here. Make a model of the kinds of homes they used. Use your clay. Why do you think they had this type of home? Can you think of five reasons why they would be very practical? Use some toothpicks to make the homes more realistic.

7.   Sitting Bull was a great Indian chief. He finally signed a peace treaty with the army. There were many wars between the Indians and settlers. Most of these were the settlers' fault because they would fail to keep the reservation boundaries. They would just help themselves to the land they wanted. Organize a debate which considers the Indians' and settlers' viewpoints.

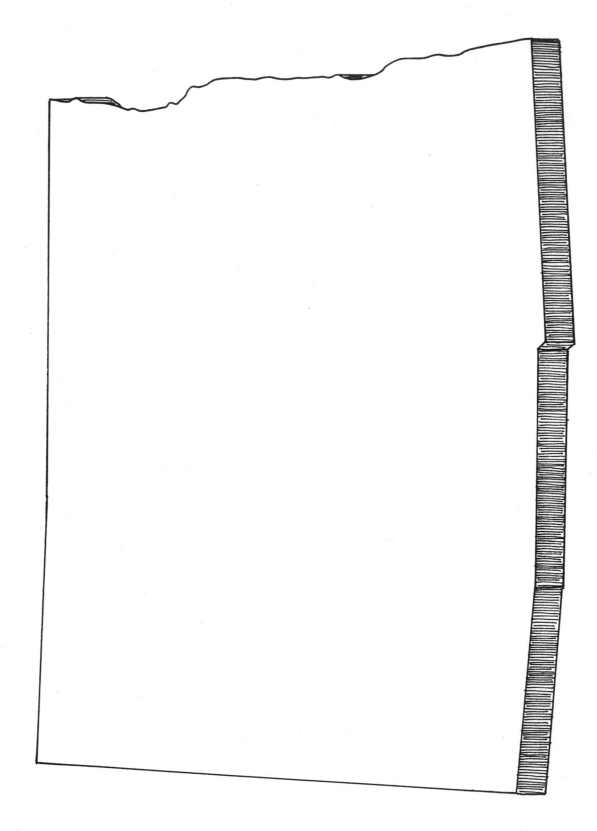

NORTH DAKOTA

OHIO

Cities
Hillsboro
Toledo
Cincinnati
Ada
Cleveland
Youngstown
Columbus
Tiro

Rivers
Miami
Muskingum
Grand
Yellow (Creek)
Ohio
Kokosing
Tiffin
Hocking

Minerals
Coal
Iron
Gas
Oil
Limestone

															C	G
													A	I	N	
											T	R	L	N	I	
N	G	B	U	C	K	E	Y	E			T	N	T	U	C	K
W	E	R	A	W	A	L	E	D	O	A	T	S	H	A	A	L	M	I	C
O	O	S	A	N	O	R	U	H	S	E	H	O	T	F	R	A	I	N	O
T	R	E	R	N	B	U	D	E	A	A	E	I	D	T	G	O	N	N	H
S	O	C	G	A	D	A	Y	I	Y	R	O	N	S	N	I	C	U	A
G	B	L	L	K	C	A	G	E	N	N	R	A	W	L	A	H	M	T
N	S	N	E	E	H	O	L	D	G	A	G	I	D	A	O	Y	M	I
U	L	I	N	D	O	L	L	N	P	N	L	N	S	P	H	C	W	R
O	L	F	N	D	O	E	I	U	I	I	A	I	E	O	K	S	M	O
Y	I	F	R	W	I	D	T	S	M	L	Y	W	M	I	N	U	B	C
O	H	I	O	F	R	N	O	E	E	B	E	S	N	A	G	U	O
M	C	T	R	A	A	K	S	V	E	L	U	L	E	N	I	R
H	O	A	H	M	O	T	E	L	L	G	E	S	I	L	N	M
S	G	U	T	K	O	L	P	A	A	Y	T	K	D
		N	N	C	A	I	R	O	N	S	E
		E	D	M	R	E	B	B	U	R	D
					M	E	Y	S
						E

Products
Aluminum
Corn
Maple Sugar (2)
Hay
Rye
Cars
Keds
Rubber
Oats

Famous People
Grant
Harding
Harrison
Putnam
Glenn
Hayes
McKinley
Garfield
Goodrich
Taft

Indians
Hopewell
Mound Builder (2)
Delaware
Shawnee
Wyandot
Huron

State Symbols
Bird: Cardinal
Flower: (Scarlet) Carnation
Tree: Buckeye

Please put the leftover letters all in a row.
When you do, the state nickname will show.

103

35

OHIO

OBJECTIVES: To improve geographical knowledge of the state of Ohio.

To cultivate research skills.

To enrich political knowledge of Ohio.

MATERIALS: An encyclopedia, coat hanger, string, blank paper, crayons, and cardboard.

PROCEDURE:

1. Do the word search and find the nickname of Ohio.

2. From the word search put in the listed cities and rivers on the blank map on the following page. Put in ten more cities and four more rivers.

3. Make a legend for the minerals and products. Add these to the map.

4. Ohio is also known as "The Mother of Presidents." Only Virginia has had more. Make a mobile with one circle for each of the eight. Be sure to put their names, birthplaces, and years in office on each one. Use a coat hanger and string to suspend it.

5. The Indian Mounds near Hillsboro are very interesting. Illustrate them on a large sheet of cardboard, and add a short explanation at the bottom.

6. Prepare materials for a bulletin board that will show Ohio's many inventors: Ritty, Custer, Kettering, Goodrich and the Wright brothers. Illustrate each invention and put a short little story about it at the bottom of the picture.

7. Ohio has a strange shape. Trace it on another piece of paper and see if you can devise something else out of it.

OHIO

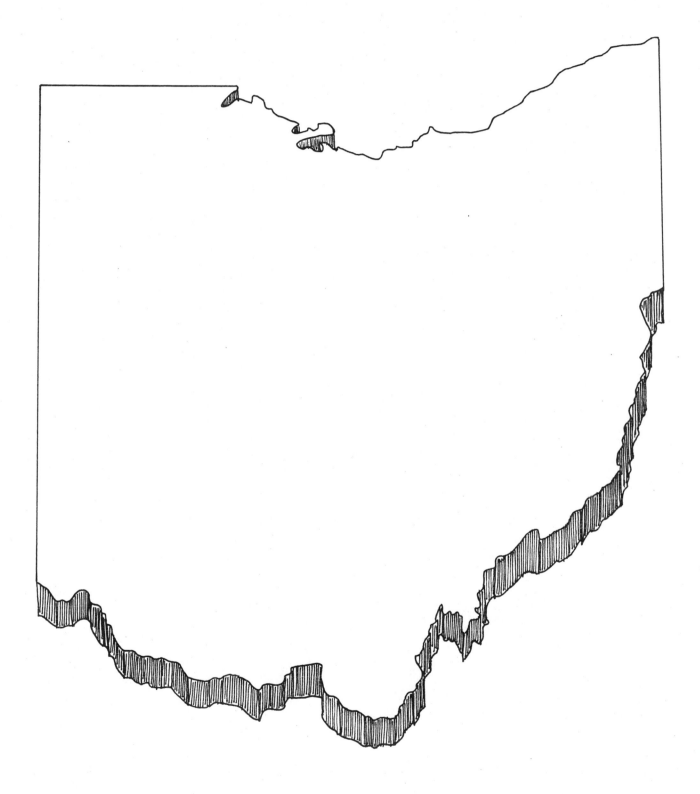

OKLAHOMA

Word search grid:

```
R E T A W L L I T S C I S S O R W H E A T O M B D
A M O H A L K O R S S T O N E R A S L U T O E O
          S S O R U Y C O E C N A N M U I L E H C
          H A Y N B N D H O E N R E D L I H F E I
          E G A E I A C T E R G O E S A L T S B T
          E A Z N T T A O R T O N T L B K K A Y
          P N T O A O D C N E O O K A N E L I R W
          S A R C N R M U L A R K W S E E H U L A
          O O Y A H O K T B R D T E R U C P C E S
          C L S N O S A D O I C E I M R R Y A
          F H E R E I C M N N E L A M B Y R D A K
            B A M N I T O S A R A N E O S H O C
            D C I N A Y A I V S R E G O R I
                      D W K S E M I N O L E H
                                            C
```

Cities
Chelsea
Tulsa
Eva
Troy
Nash
Stillwater
Elk (City)
Oklahoma City (2)
Enid
Tom
Muskogee
Non
Lawton

Rivers
Arkansas
Red
Cimarron
Kiamichi
Canadian
Washita
Blue
Neosho

Famous People
Coronado
Payne
Carpenter
Byrd
Rogers
Ross

Indians
Osage
Cherokee
Choctaw
Seminole
Chickasaw

Minerals
Zinc
Lead
Clay
Stone
Helium
Oil
Gas

Products
Broomcorn   Cotton
Peanuts   Oat
Barley   Salt
Beef   Hay
Wheat   Nut
Sheep

State Symbols
Bird: Scissor-Tailed Flycatcher (3)
Flower: Mistletoe
Tree: Rosebud

Put the unused letters on the blanks below.
When you are done, the state nickname you'll know.

The __he__ ___ ___ State

106

36

OKLAHOMA

OBJECTIVES: To improve geographical knowledge of Oklahoma.

To promote research skills.

To encourage study of natural phenomena found in Oklahoma.

MATERIALS: An encyclopedia, a large map of North America, drawing paper, colors, and clay.

PROCEDURE:

1. Do the word search and find the state nickname.

2. On the map on the following page, please put in the rivers and cities listed in the search. Put in ten more cities of your own choice and five more rivers or lakes.

3. Put in the mountain ranges. Make a legend for the minerals and products listed in the search. Add five more products of your own choosing.

4. On the large map of North America, please put in the Chisholm Trail, Santa Fe Trail, and the Oregon Trail. Why were they important? Who used them? Were there any other famous trails? Please put them in, too. Then add the Butterfield Stage Line.

5. There were five Indian nations in Oklahoma. Please find where they lived. Make a legend, and add them to your map on the next page.

6. The Butterfield Stage Line was one of the first in our country. Make a model of a coach and its horses out of clay.

7. Research the "Boomers." In a short report tell their story.

8. Will Rogers was a unique individual. Make a skit with a friend about some incident in his life.

OKLAHOMA

OREGON

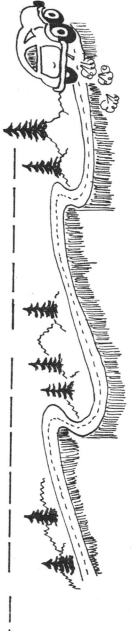

Put the unused letters on the blanks below.
If done correctly, the nickname will show.

_ _ _ _ _ _ _ _ _ _ _ _ _ _ _ _ _ _

Word Search Grid:

```
                H I M N A H A M A
              N A B A Y E I L
            I H O J R R U E
        C K C I N H O E P H
      E A S I L V E R C O
    E C L A R K U T L A O
  R G S L A C N S B K B R S L R O
Y M E E T I O N K I A E Y A I G D E W
R I C H O L T O D W U L R M N H E A I
R N E L U P O E A E G A T S Y H L
E T S M O M N E L I M E M I R N A Y L V
B K B A U E A L Y E R O M E A D O W A E
D W I A L L W G I H C L R T O W B S S D O M U
L A M L N P G T H A C T O L A S T O R E G
O R I E O S A U H L L A L H P E S O J T E
G T I R E M O E O U I F E I H C T A W N T N
S T F U K N D M D T N R E T S E W E B E E
```

Cities
Salem
Bay (City)
Portland
Eugene
Newport
Albany
Newberg
Post
Astoria

Rivers
Columbia
Hood
Snake
Willamette
John Day (2)
Owyhee
Nehalem
Imnaha

Indians
Tillamook
Bannock
Cayuse
Umatilla
Klamath
Clackama
Multnomah

Minerals
Diatomite
Mercury
Nickel
Perlite
Silver
Uranium
Lead
Lime
Gold
Stone

Products
Strawberry
Peppermint
Bee
Pea
Flowers
Wood
Sod
Rye

Famous People
Champoeg
Luelling
McLoughlin
Chief Joseph (2)
Lewis
Clark
Gray
Meek
Astor
Lee

State Symbols
Bird: Western Meadow Lark (3)
Flower: (Oregon) Grape
Tree: Douglas Fir (2)

37

OREGON

OBJECTIVES: To improve geographical knowledge of Oregon.

To improve research skills.

To promote awareness of natural phenomena of Oregon.

MATERIALS: An encyclopedia, jar lids, clear food wrap, rubber bands, small beads, crayons, scissors, cardboard, flour, and salt.

PROCEDURE:

1. Do the word search and find the state's nickname.

2. On the following page is a blank map of the state. Please put the cities that are listed in the word search on the map. Then draw in the rivers. Put in five more cities of your own choice, as well as the mountain ranges and four lakes found here.

3. Make symbols for the products and minerals listed in the search. Put these on the map.

4. On a different sheet, trace the shape of the state. Paste this on cardboard. Using two parts flour to one part salt, add a little water until the mixture is a doughy texture. Shape in the mountains and rivers. Let it dry overnight; then paint and label the various physical features of the state: rivers, lakes, plains, and lowlands.

5. There are "Salmon Ladders" in Oregon. Research these. Where are they? Are they important? Why? Using another small circle of cardboard, draw three salmon on the circle. Using the scissors, make a little hole in each fish's eye. Paste the cardboard in the jar lid. Put in three little beads. Put the clear wrap over the top of the lid and fasten it with the rubber band. Now see if you can get the little beads in the fishes' eyes. Have a friend make one, too. See which of you can get the eyes in the fish first.

6. Crater Lake is the deepest lake in the United States. It is located in the crater of Mount Mazama. This is one of the scenic wonders of the world. There are no known outlets and no streams flowing into it. Research Crater Lake. Who found it? How deep is it? How big is it? How was it formed? Make a report to share with your class. Illustrate it, also.

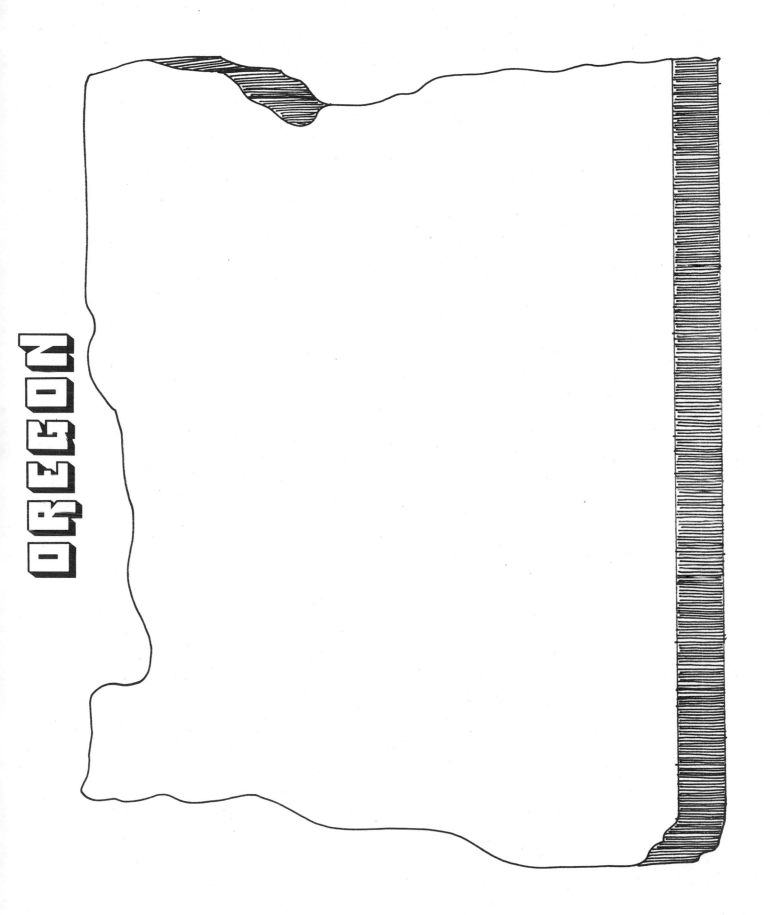

OREGON

PENNSYLVANIA

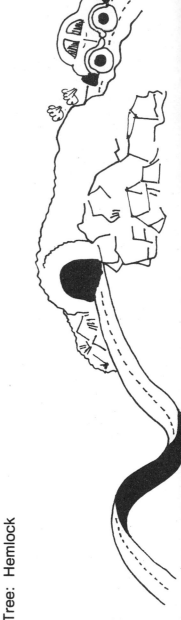

```
          P   K
P  E  N  L  O  Y  A  L  H  A  N  N  A  I  K  N  O  G  L  A
I  A  L  E  G  H  E  N  Y  H  O  G  E  L  I  T  X  E  T  I
T  E  N  O  S  L  N  W  O  T  N  E  L  L  A  C  O  A  L  H  C
T  N  L  I  P  H  D  R  N  E  N  O  T  S  E  M  I  L  A  P  O  Y
S  K  D  A  L  E  A  A  U  I  C  D  S  G  S  R  I  R  C  L  R
B  O  C  M  N  F  K  R  W  A  H  E  L  N  I  O  K  R  E  O  E  N
U  C  S  O  F  A  C  N  T  N  L  P  I  A  Q  L  I  O  S  P  D  L
R  I  Y  U  L  S  H  N  A  A  E  D  L  U  Y  S  V  N  U  P  A  A
G  T  R  M  I  M  U  C  W  R  A  E  O  U  B  T  O  E  O  E  L  U
H  N  U  I  O  E  A  U  E  F  I  H  U  S  A  G  N  R  R  I  R  A
E  A  P  C  M  R  R  H  R  B  S  C  R  M  O  N  O  N  G  A  H  E  L  A
A  N  A  H  E  U  Q  S  U  S  G  G  E  C  A  I  T  N  O  P  L
```

Cities
Harrisburg
Philadelphia
Pittsburgh
Scranton
Allentown
Reading

Rivers and Lakes
Allegheny
Delaware
Schuylkill
Monongahela
Susquehanna
Loyalhanna (Lake)

Indians
Algonkian
Iroquois
Nanticoke
Shawnee

Products
Textile Pea
Hog   Corn
Eggs
Maple Syrup (2)

Famous People
Penn
Buchanan
Franklin
Pontiac

Minerals
Coal   Clay
Copper   Silver
Gas   Oil
Mica   Gold Ore (2)
Iron   Peat
Sulphur Limestone

State Symbols
Bird: Ruffed Grouse
Flower: Mountain Laurel (2)
Tree: Hemlock

If you put the unused letters on the blanks below,
The state's nickname you'll come to know.

The State

The _e _ _ _ _ _ State

38

PENNSYLVANIA

OBJECTIVES: To increase geographical knowledge of Pennsylvania.

To encourage research skills.

To promote interest in historical knowledge of Pennsylvania.

MATERIALS: An encyclopedia, large poster board, and crayons.

PROCEDURE: 1.   Do the word search and find the state's nickname.

2.   Please put the listed cities and rivers on the blank map on the following page. Draw in the rivers. Add five cities and three rivers of your own choosing.

3.   Make a legend of the minerals and products for the state. Use the listed ones from the word search. Put these in on the map on the following page.

4.   Pennsylvania has the most anthracite coal mines in the nation. Make a large poster with illustrations showing the steps used in mining and preparing the coal for use. List the advantages and disadvantages of this type of coal at the bottom of the poster.

5.   Ben Franklin was a truly great man of the revolutionary period. Make a time line of his life. Be sure you include some of his many inventions.

6.   Pennsylvania originated in a very different way than the other colonies. Research its beginning. Make a report on it to share with your class.

7.   The Declaration of Independence as well as the Constitution of our country were formulated in Pennsylvania. Pretend you are a reporter. Interview one of the representatives and with a friend make a tape of it to share with your class. Be sure to remember the five good questions of reporting: how, when, where, why, and what. Why didn't they outlaw slavery then? Why is the Liberty Bell so famous?

8.   Why was the Mason-Dixon Line important? When was it formulated? How did it get its name? Make a skit with a friend explaining these facts.

PENNSYLVANIA

RHODE ISLAND

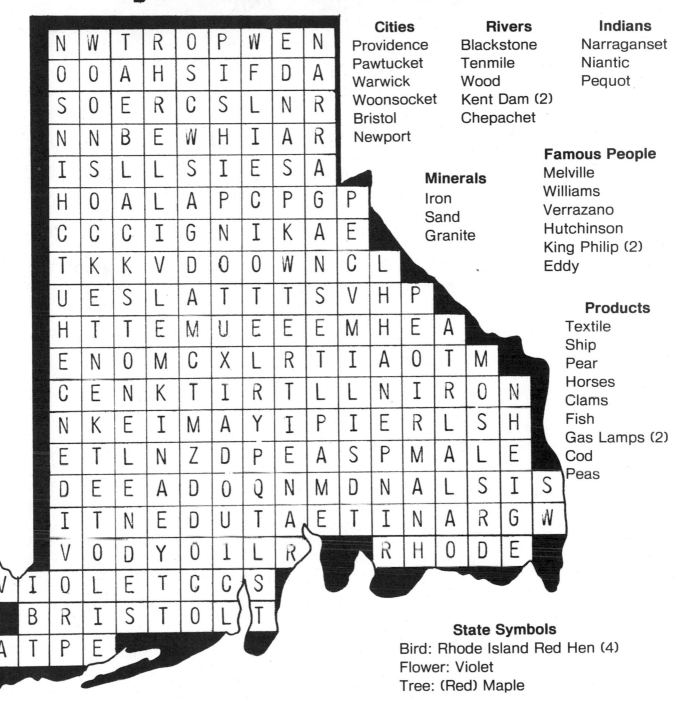

The word search grid contains the following letters (rows):

```
N W T R O P W E N
O O A H S I F D A
S O E R C S L N R
N N B E W H I A R
I S L L S I E S A
H O A L A P C P G P
C C C I G N I K A E
T K K V D O O W N C L
U E S L A T T S V H P
H T T E M U E E E M H E A
E N O M C X L R T I A O T M
C E N K T I R T L L N I R O N
N K E I M A Y I P I E R L S H
E T L N Z D P E A S P M A L E
D E E A D O Q N M D N A L S I S
I T N E D U T A E T I N A R G W
V O D Y O I L R     R H O D E
V I O L E T C C S
B R I S T O L T
A T P E
```

Cities
Providence
Pawtucket
Warwick
Woonsocket
Bristol
Newport

Rivers
Blackstone
Tenmile
Wood
Kent Dam (2)
Chepachet

Indians
Narraganset
Niantic
Pequot

Minerals
Iron
Sand
Granite

Famous People
Melville
Williams
Verrazano
Hutchinson
King Philip (2)
Eddy

Products
Textile
Ship
Pear
Horses
Clams
Fish
Gas Lamps (2)
Cod
Peas

State Symbols
Bird: Rhode Island Red Hen (4)
Flower: Violet
Tree: (Red) Maple

Please put the leftover letters on the blanks below.
If they are in order, the state nickname will show.

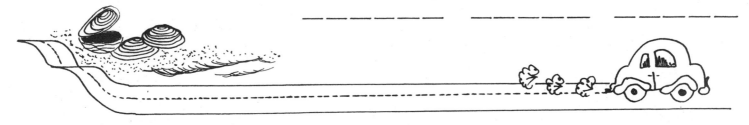

__ __ __ __ __ __ __ __ __ __ __ __ __ __ __

39

RHODE ISLAND

OBJECTIVES: To improve geographical knowledge of Rhode Island.

To encourage research skills.

To arouse interest in career opportunities.

MATERIALS: An encyclopedia, cardboard, yarn, safety pins, needle, thread, glue, old wallpaper samples or material, and scissors.

PROCEDURE:
1. Do the word search and find the nickname of Rhode Island.

2. On the following page is a blank map. Put in the cities and rivers listed in the word search on it. Then, find the names of five of the islands. Put these in.

3. Make a legend for the products and minerals listed in the word search. Put these on the map.

4. Find where the famous people worked and influenced the state. Put their names in where they were important.

5. Jewelry making is one of the principal manufacturing activities. Find a pattern that you like about three inches across. Cut out two pieces of cardboard. A circle is very nice. Sew a safety pin to the back of your little piece of "jewelry." Cover the front with material or wallpaper. Make a nice design on this piece of cardboard. Using a large needle and yarn, whip the two pieces together. Whipping means you sew over and over around the edge. You keep the stitches the same size and always start on the back. Now you have your own unique piece of jewelry.

6. Rhode Island is a vacation land to many people. Make a brochure advertising the recreation facilities many tourists enjoy.

7. Roger Williams greatly influenced Rhode Island. Find out his ideas and write an essay, your opinion, on his philosophy. How was it like the other colonies? How was it different?

RHODE ISLAND

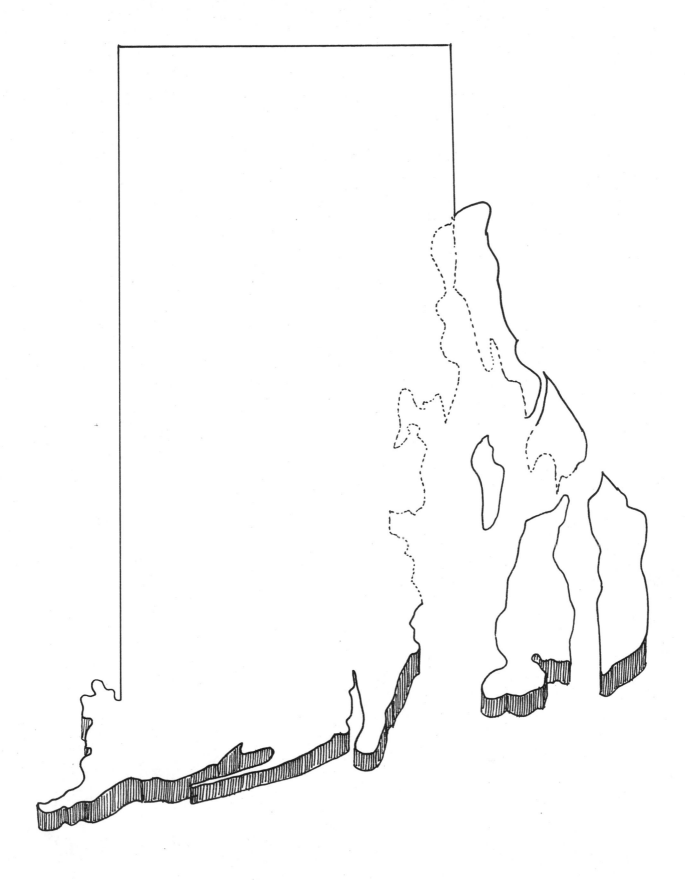

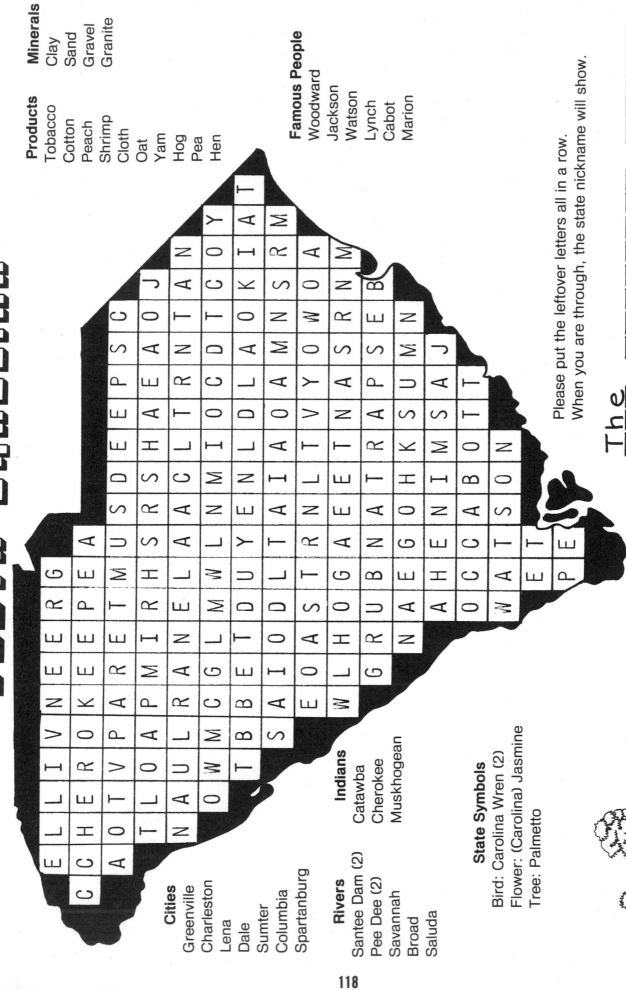

SOUTH CAROLINA

Products
Tobacco
Cotton
Peach
Shrimp
Cloth
Oat
Yam
Hog
Pea
Hen

Minerals
Clay
Sand
Gravel
Granite

Famous People
Woodward
Jackson
Watson
Lynch
Cabot
Marion

Cities
Greenville
Charleston
Lena
Dale
Sumter
Columbia
Spartanburg

Rivers
Santee Dam (2)
Pee Dee (2)
Savannah
Broad
Saluda

Indians
Catawba
Cherokee
Muskhogean

State Symbols
Bird: Carolina Wren (2)
Flower: (Carolina) Jasmine
Tree: Palmetto

Please put the leftover letters all in a row.
When you are through, the state nickname will show.

The _ _ _ _ _ _ _ _ _ _

118

40

SOUTH CAROLINA

OBJECTIVES: To improve geographical knowledge of South Carolina.

To encourage research skills.

To promote historical knowledge of South Carolina.

MATERIALS: An encyclopedia, paper straws, glue, cardboard, tongue depressors, clay, watercolors, cellophane, string, shoe box, and old magazines.

PROCEDURE: 1.   Do the word search and find the nickname of the state.

2.   On the following page is a blank map. Locate the cities and rivers listed in the search and put them on the map. Add five more cities of your own choosing. Draw in three more rivers. Shade in the mountain ranges, also.

3.   Make a legend for the minerals and products listed with the search and put these on your map. Find where the Indian tribes lived and color in their territories.

4.   Enhance your map by locating where the famous people were born. Add their names to their birthplaces.

5.   Fort Sumter and Fort Moultrie are in Charleston Harbor. They were very important in two wars. Find out which ones. Make a model of Fort Moultrie with straws placed on cardboard. Paint the grass and water on the harbor, so it looks real. Write a short report on the two forts, explaining how each was important in a war.

6.   Rice was first raised successfully in South Carolina. Who did this? Illustrate rice at three stages of its growth. What kind of climate does it need? How is it harvested? How is it processed? Make a diorama with a shoe box, clay, watercolors, and tongue depressors showing how tobacco is dried.

7.   Andrew Jackson was a very colorful President. Read his life story. Pick an incident that you find interesting and make a poster about it.

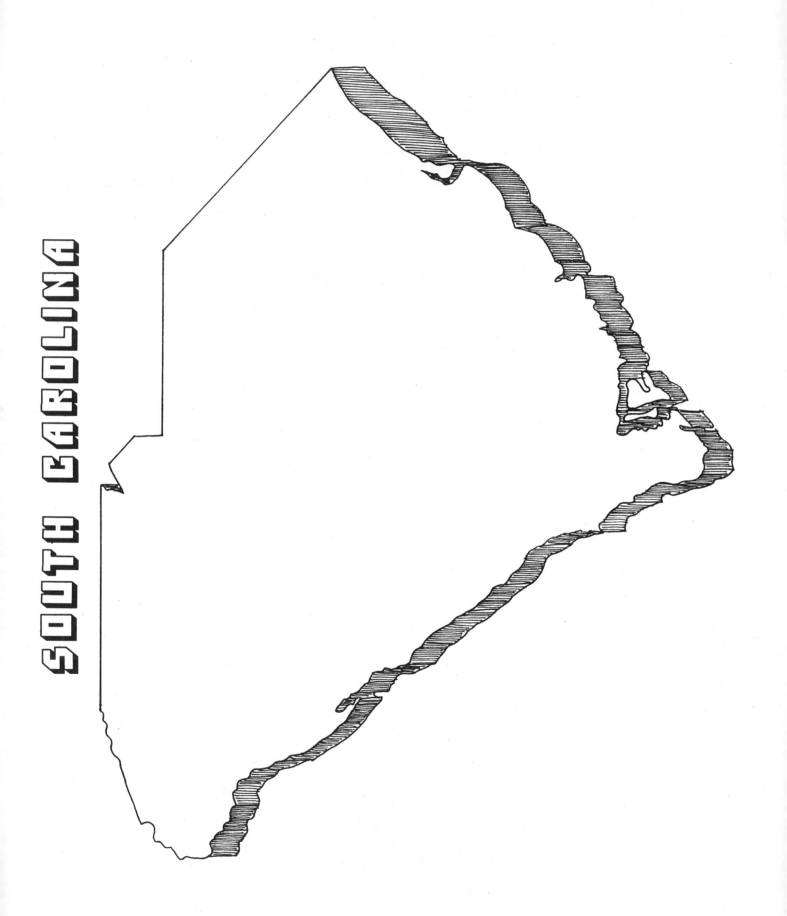

SOUTH CAROLINA

SOUTH DAKOTA

Minerals

Gold Ore (2)
Clay
Lead
Stone
Uranium
Feldspar
Sand
Oil
Mica

W	M	B	D	E	K	C	E	N	G	N	I	R	T	N	A	S	A	E	H	P
H	L	I	C	E	B	U	L	L	S	I	O	U	X	R	A	P	I	D	D	D
E	A	G	S	A	A	L	F	A	L	F	A	M	I	C	A	S	T	L	E	N	P
A	V	T	C	S	L	D	A	F	Y	S	L	S	H	E	E	P	O	H	U	A	A
T	A	E	T	R	O	A	W	C	E	L	L	A	R	I	N	G	S	E	O	R	S
O	M	O	R	E	A	U	M	O	K	E	S	L	X	E	N	H	C	D	I	G	Q
S	N	G	Y	E	R	Z	R	I	O	A	B	H	E	I	T	U	I	K	L	K	U
E	I	R	S	A	N	D	Y	I	T	D	N	D	T	H	R	L	A	L	O	E	E
N	J	A	N	E	E	D	L	I	W	Y	R	T	O	P	C	R	E	K	L	Y	F
N	B	I	L	L	H	O	R	S	E	E	I	R	S	C	A	T	C	V	T	S	L
I	U	N	O	T	K	N	A	Y	B	S	E	K	C	O	R	I	I	A	O	O
M	N	A	C	I	R	E	M	A	E	N	N	E	Y	E	H	C	C	M	Y	C	W

(extra boxes: O P I E R R E · T E · R)

State Symbols

Bird: Ring-Necked Pheasant (3)
Flower: American Pasqueflower (2)
Tree: Black Hills Spruce (3)

Famous People

Sitting Bull (2)
Wild Bill Hickok (3)
Cavelier
Deadwood (Dick)
La Vérendrye (2)
Crazy Horse (2)
Calamity Jane (2)

Cities

Pierre
Castle Rock (2)
Aberdeen
Lead
Rapid City (2)
Yankton
Mitchell

Rivers

Missouri
Minnesota
Grand
Moreau
Big Sioux (2)

Indians

Arikara
Cheyenne

Products

Beef   Sheep
Alfalfa   Oats
Flax   Hog
Rye   Wheat
Grain

Put the unused letters all in a row.
If you are right, the state nicknames will show.

The _ _ _ _ _ _ _ _

and _ _ _ _ _ _ _ _ State

121

41

SOUTH DAKOTA

OBJECTIVES: To improve geographical knowledge of South Dakota.

To promote research skills.

To enrich knowledge of South Dakota's natural phenomena.

MATERIALS: An encyclopedia, cardboard, and a paper brad for a spinner.

PROCEDURE:

1. Do the word search and find the nicknames of the state. See if you can find the reason the state got both nicknames.

2. On the page following is a blank map of the state. Please locate the listed cities and draw in the rivers. Find five more cities to add as well as three more rivers. Put these in, also.

3. Make a legend for the listed minerals and products of South Dakota. Add these to your map. Add the Badlands, Mount Rushmore, and the Black Hills.

4. There were many coyotes in South Dakota. Investigate their life story. Find a good picture and copy it to illustrate them. Make a report on them. Include their habitat, food, where they like to live, their enemies, how they defend themselves, and how many young they have at once. Add any interesting facts you find. What kind of a reputation do they have? How do you think they got it? What kind of an animal are they?

5. The Black Hills contain the greatest gold-producing mine in the Western Hemisphere. Make a gameboard for you and a friend to play. Include such things as go ahead one space, you found signs of gold in the stream; skip a turn, your donkey got loose in the night; have an extra turn, you found an Indian who gave you directions; go back two spaces, you ran into a rock slide; go back to the beginning, you ran out of food; go ahead two spaces, you can go downhill for five miles; skip a turn, you sighted unfriendly Indians; take an extra turn, you met a prospector who'd made a strike; lose a turn, your dynamite got wet; finish, you found gold.

6. The Badlands are a unique land formation. What kinds of geological processes caused them? On a large piece of paper illustrate the various influences that caused them.

7. Calamity Jane was an important part of South Dakota's history. Draw six pictures illustrating important events in her life.

8. Mount Rushmore is very famous as a tourist attraction. Find out where you can write for free brochures. Send for them and share them with your class.

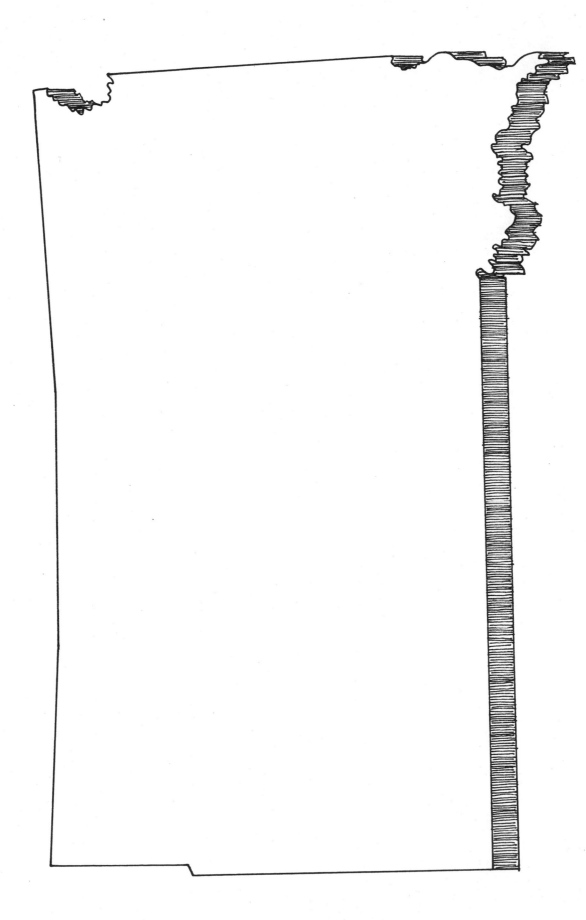

SOUTH DAKOTA

TENNESSEE

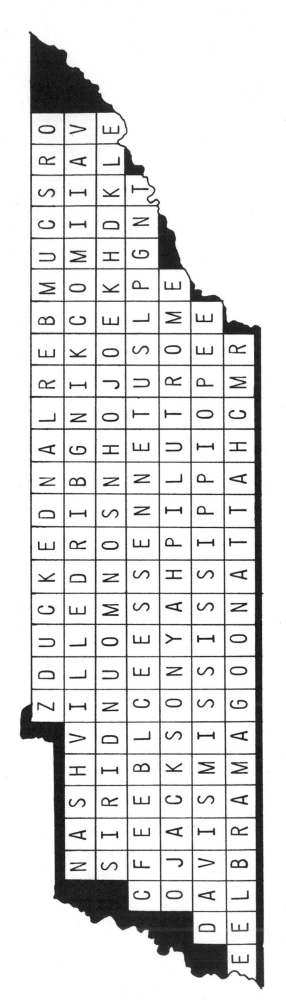

Cities
Nashville
Chattanooga
Memphis
Oak Ridge (2)

Rivers
Tennessee
Mississippi
Cumberland
Elk
Duck

Indians
Mound (Builders)

Famous People
Davis
Polk
Johnson
Jackson

Products
Beef
Horse
Hay

Minerals
Coal
Zinc Ore (2)
Marble

State Symbols
Bird: Mockingbird
Flower: Iris
Tree: Tulip (Popular)

Put the unused letters on the blanks below.
When you're through, the state nickname you'll know.

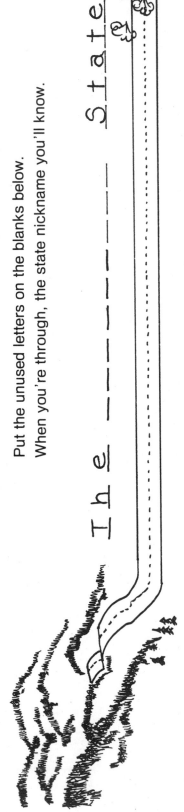

The _ _ _ _ _ _ _ State

124

42

TENNESSEE

OBJECTIVES: To improve geographical knowledge of Tennessee.

To promote research skills.

To encourage understanding of Tennessee's cultural heritage.

MATERIALS: An encyclopedia, old magazines, scissors, glue, and cardboard.

PROCEDURE:

1.   Do the word search and find the state nickname.

2.   On the following page is a blank map of Tennessee. Locate the cities listed in the word search and put them in. Add five cities of your own choosing. Draw in the rivers listed, also. Put in three more of your own choice.

3.   Make a legend for the products and minerals listed. Put these on the map.

4.   There are some famous mountain ranges. Color these in on your map.

5.   TVA provides electricity and prevents flooding. Find out more about it. Draw an illustration showing how it works.

6.   Nashville is the "home" of country music. This is one of the few truly American art forms. Choose one of the famous singers. Make a time line of his life story.

7.   Daniel Boone was one of our most famous frontiersmen. He was an expert marksman. Make your own game of hunting by cutting out animals that were in our forests. Include wild turkeys, geese, ducks, and other game that were used for eating. Divide a piece of cardboard into sections. Nine would be fine. In each space draw or cut out a picture of an animal: a bear, deer, fox, wolf, rabbit, or other animal found here. Draw a line at the bottom of the cardboard. Taking turns with different colored buttons, "shoot" your meal for the week. Take turns and snap the button with your fingers. Play for five minutes and see who is the best hunter. If it lands on a line, it doesn't count.

TENNESSEE

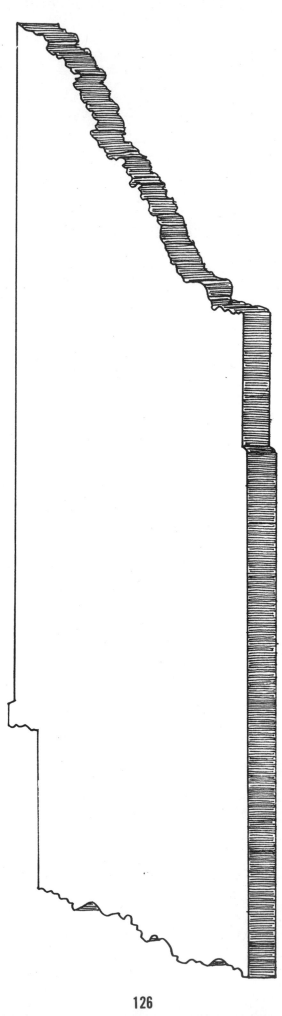

TEXAS

Cities
Austin
Dallas
Houston
El Paso (2)
Waco
Lubbock
Van

Rivers
Rio Grande (2)
Pecos
Brazos
Sabine
Trinity
Canadian
Colorado
Red

						B	O	C	A	W												
						L	S	A	L	T												
						U	A	V	A	N												
						E	P	E	C	O	S											
						B	N	L	U	B	B	O	C	K	S	A	L	L	A	D		
						O	T	I	I	G	D	R	I	B	G	N	I	K	C	O	M	
						N	P	E	B	M	R	T	A	N	O	S	N	H	O	J	H	
						N	M	R	A	A	E	A	T	Z	W	O	R	E	L	Y	T	
						E	I	Y	B	A	S	S	N	E	O	O	E	A	O	I	R	
L	N	A	C	E	P	T	R	I	N	I	T	Y	T	D	K	S	O	D	R	C	O	R
		I	A	P	A	C	H	E	K	C	A	D	D	O	E	C	A	L	A	B	E	E
			T	A	O	G	S	O	H	O	U	S	T	O	N	N	O	N	D	W	N	D
				S	O	O	K	R	I	C	E	S	O	T	O	E	A	R	O	E	N	
				H	U	R	E	P	E	A	N	U	T	R	D	D	S	H	C			
					A	A					T	A	O	N	I	O	N	H				
											N	C	M	A	E	E	E					
												A	N	O	S							
													S	I	C	S						
													E	O	A	A						
														G	N	R						
																I						

Indians
Caddo
Nasoni
Neche
Apache
Arkokisa
Comanche

Products
Shrimp
Peanut
Onion
Rice
Yam
Hog
Goat
Wool
Bee

Famous People
Eisenhower
Johnson
Coronado
Cavelier
Bass
Tyler
Dies
Crockett
De Soto (2)

Minerals
Limestone Ore (2)
Salt
Gas
Oil
Coal

Please put the leftover letters all in a row.
When you are through, the state nickname will show.

___ _____ State

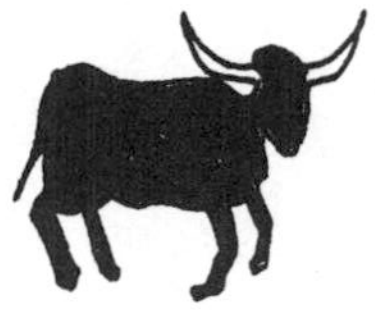

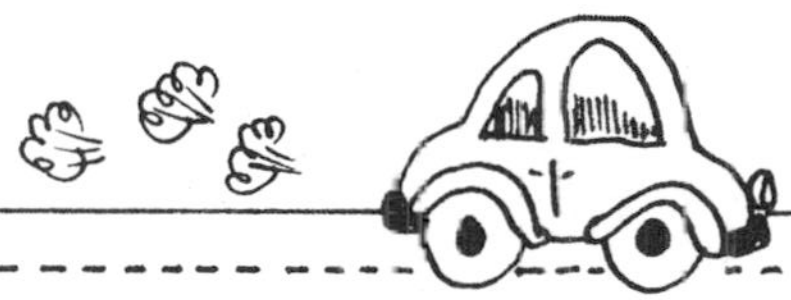

State Symbols
Bird: Mockingbird
Flower: Bluebonnet
Tree: Pecan

43

TEXAS

OBJECTIVES: To enrich geographical knowledge of Texas.

To improve research skills.

To promote interest in the political background of Texas.

MATERIALS: An encyclopedia, coat hanger, string, scissors, paper, crayons, and glue.

PROCEDURE: 1.   Do the word search and find the nickname of Texas.

2.   On the following page is a blank map of Texas. Using the listed rivers and cities from the word search as a beginning, locate fifteen cities and draw in the rivers.

3.   Make a legend for the products and minerals listed. Put these on your map, also. Color in the territories the Indians occupied.

4.   Choose one of the famous people listed. Look up a biography of this person. Write a report to share with your class.

5.   Six Flags, the amusement park, started in Texas. Trace the state from the page that follows. Make six copies. Fill in the state with a scene that might have taken place as each nation owned it. Suspend these as a mobile. You might use a coat hanger. On the other side reproduce the flag of the nation this scene represents.

6.   Another strictly American art form is the story of the ''super hero.'' Pecos Bill is one such hero. Find out how he got his horse, ''Widow Maker.'' Make up a tall tale of your own about this folk hero.

7.   The King Ranch is one of the largest ranches in Texas. Pretend you are a reporter and interview a ranch hand. Ask what he usually does in a typical day. Contrast this with what you think a ranch hand did one hundred years ago.

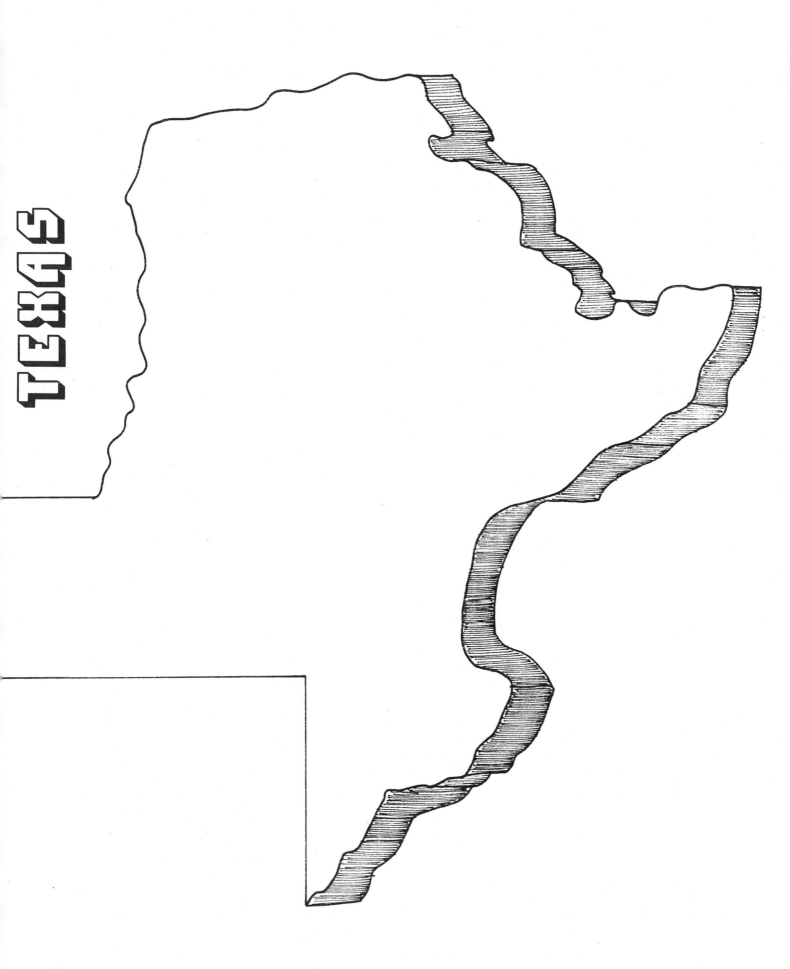

UTAH

D	L	E	I	F	H	C	I	R							
P	T	C	E	B	L	C	E	O							
U	A	E	H	E	A	G	I	Y							
M	B	I	V	E	D	R	E	T							
A	G	A	U	I	R	B	L	O	Y	O	C	L	I	F	F
H	R	N	R	T	S	R	S	E	R	W	H	I	T	E	R
G	A	B	U	L	E	H	Y	E	Y	G	N	A	U	J	E
I	I	S	O	O	O	H	E	D	A	L	E	S	V	K	M
R	N	G	U	S	Y	D	T	E	L	F	I	L	A	A	O
B	A	E	H	G	W	B	U	I	P	O	L	L	E	L	N
N	R	O	B	E	A	R	E	E	M	W	G	A	S	A	T
H	N	O	L	H	A	R	I	E	V	S	A	N	F	B	D
I	S	L	W	N	A	E	C	I	T	Y	N	L	E	L	N
N	E	T	I	N	C	W	O	S	S	E	G	O	K	U	A
R	E	U	A	I	D	K	E	E	G	S	P	R	E	L	
O	M	D	R	N	A	N	O	R	O	R	O	A	S	I	R
B	V	P	G	R	F	T	G	S	W	U	E	E	I	K	E
A	S	O	O	O	A	O	I	U	L	E	V	V	C	N	H
O	T	L	R	T	I	U	R	T	L	I	B	A	L	A	T
M	O	T	O	P	T	L	R	D	E	L	L	E	E	I	U
C	O	P	P	E	R	Y	R	R	E	B	W	A	R	T	S

Cities
Brigham City (2)
Provo
Richfield
Salt Lake City (3)
Moab

Ogden
Logan
Saint George (2)
Roy

State Symbols
Bird: Sea Gull (2)
Flower: Sego Lily (2)
Tree: Blue Spruce (2)

Indians
Cliff Dweller (2)
Gosiute
Paiute
Shoshoni
Ute
Navaho

Rivers
Sevier
Fremont
White
Green
Strawberry
Bear
Colorado
Weber
San Juan (2)

Minerals
Copper
Uranium
Gold Ore (2)
Silver
Gravel
Lead
Oil
Gas
Iron

Products
Sheep
Cherry
Beef
Alfalfa
Poultry
Barley
Potatoes
Sugar Beet (2)
Grain

Famous People
Sutherland
Browning
Stanford
Smith
Young
Bridger
Walker
Black Hawk (2)

Put the unused letters all in a row.
If you are right, the state nickname will show.

The ___ ___ ___ ___ ___ ___ ___ ___

130

44

UTAH

OBJECTIVES: To improve geographical knowledge of Utah.

To encourage research skills.

To promote understanding of natural phenomena of Utah.

MATERIALS: An encyclopedia, one cup of salt, two cups of flour, two or three tablespoons of water, cardboard, watercolors, and a large United States map.

PROCEDURE:

1. Do the word search and find the nickname.

2. On the following page is a blank map of the state. Locate the cities and rivers listed in the word search. Add five more cities of your choosing. Draw in the rivers. Put in the mountain ranges, also.

3. Make a legend for the products and minerals named. Add these to your own map. Color in the territories of the Indian tribes. Then put in the famous people names where they influenced Utah.

4. Using the blank map as your guide, trace the shape onto the cardboard. Consult the physical map in the encyclopedia. Make a salt and flour mixture. Add enough water to make it dough-like. Make the mountains, Salt Lake, and the other physical features. Let it dry, then paint it in appropriate colors.

5. The great Salt Lake is unique. It is the only salt lake in our country. Research its history. Make a report on it to share with your class. Be sure you tell what effect it has now on the surrounding countryside.

6. Bees are one of the most valuable insects in our land. They are true insects. Illustrate their life stages. Tell about their social system. How long do they live? Why would Utah people think them essential? What are ''Beekeepers''? How are they important?

7. Mormons were persecuted on their way to Utah. Using a large United States map, trace their journey to Salt Lake City. Make a short history with five or six pictures. Why do you think they were driven out of so many communities?

UTAH

VERMONT

Word Search Grid:

```
N O R O B E L T T A R B
A M O N T P E L I E R
I N O T G N I L R U B
K R B A R R E G E C C B
N E O T A L C G O H L P
O L T Q L R D N A A L E
E G P A I U I C M C U N
R L A O M L O P K P
U A M E O R L I I O
T A R O D A U K S
L O C T I N A S T
A T M N H N S O O
N U E T B U P O N
D C T A C S R N E
A I T H L O I I
T A S O T N W
C W U V S G
E E R E E F
N E H R B I
N G T M S E
O G I N A L
C S W O O D
```

Cities
Rutland
Burlington
Springfield
Barre
Concord
Montpelier
Brattleboro

Rivers
Connecticut
Lamoille
Mad
Black
Mettawee
Winooski

Indians
Algonkian
Iroquois
Abnaki

Famous People
Arthur
Champlain
Coolidge

Products
Eggs
Wood
Pulp
Oat

Minerals
Talc
Asbestos Ore (2)
Stone

State Symbols
Bird: (Hermit) Thrush
Flower: (Red) Clover
Tree: (Sugar) Maple

Put the unused letters on the blanks below.
When you are through, the state nickname will show.

The ___ ___ ___ ___ ___   ___ ___ ___ ___ ___ State

133

45

VERMONT

OBJECTIVES: To improve geographical knowledge of Vermont.

To cultivate research skills.

To promote awareness of career opportunities in Vermont.

MATERIALS: An encyclopedia, cardboard, Popsicle sticks, glue, watercolors, scissors, clay, and old magazines.

PROCEDURE:
1. Do the word search and find the state nickname.

2. On the following page locate the listed cities. Add the rivers listed. Put in six more cities and three more rivers.

3. Vermont has beautiful mountain areas. Please color in the mountain ranges and name them. How do you think they affected the way men could support themselves? Cut out any pictures from the old magazines that would show how men could make a living in Vermont. Trace the map from the following page and make a collage.

4. Make a legend for the minerals and products of the state. Put them on your map with the cities and rivers.

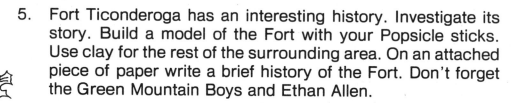

5. Fort Ticonderoga has an interesting history. Investigate its story. Build a model of the Fort with your Popsicle sticks. Use clay for the rest of the surrounding area. On an attached piece of paper write a brief history of the Fort. Don't forget the Green Mountain Boys and Ethan Allen.

6. The sugar maple tree is very important to Vermont. Using a series of illustrations, perhaps six, show the process used to make syrup from the trees.

7. Draw the state seal. Explain what the various symbols found there stand for. Add the bird, flower, and flag. Using a large cardboard, display it for your class. Explain the reasons you feel these were chosen.

VERMONT

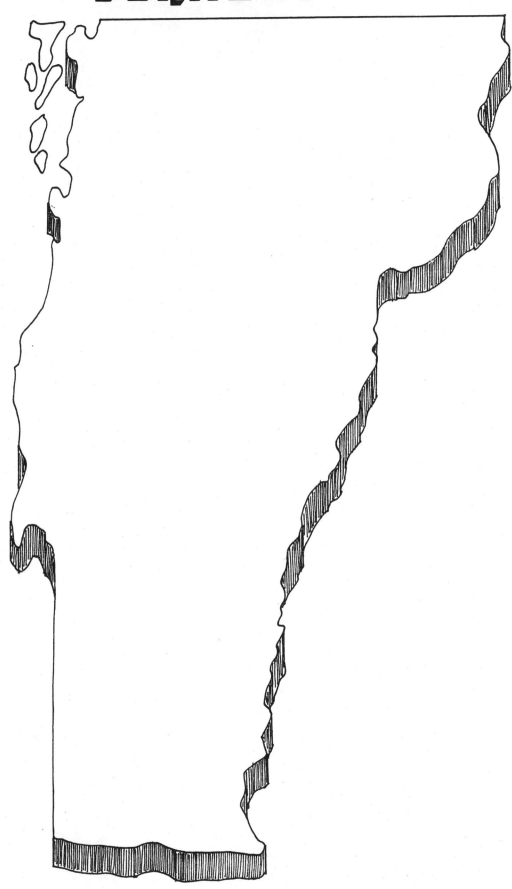

VIRGINIA

Cities
Richmond
Saxe
Yorktown
Williamsburg

Rivers
Anna
Rappahannock
Shenandoah

Minerals
Lead Ore (2)
Gypsum

Indians
Monacan

State Symbols
Bird: Cardinal
Flower: Flowering Dogwood (2)
Tree: (Flowering Dogwood)

Famous People
Washington
Jefferson
Madison
Monroe
Harrison
Tyler
Taylor
Wilson

Products
Nut
Fish
Oat
Tobacco

Virginia has three nicknames. It is the birthplace of eight Presidents. It was also a large territory and is considered "The Mother of States," as well as "The Mother of Presidents." The third nickname is the one you will find when putting the left-over letters on the blanks below.

_____ _____

46

VIRGINIA

OBJECTIVES: To enrich geographical knowledge of Virginia.

To improve research skills.

To enrich historical knowledge of Virginia.

MATERIALS: An encyclopedia, toothpicks, soap, clay, dishpan, a small, thin piece of wood, scissors, water, and a United States map.

PROCEDURE:
1. Do the word search and find the state nickname.

2. On the following page is a blank map of the state. Locate the cities listed for the word search. Put in five more of your own choice. Draw in the rivers mentioned in the search. Put in three more of your own choosing.

3. Make a legend for the products and minerals listed. Put these on the map where they are found. Put in the mountains with different colors for the different ranges.

4. Virginia was a commonwealth early in its history. On a United States map, color in the territory this included. With dotted lines show the states found in this territory now. How did this happen? How did the land become so many states? Make a short report to share with your class.

5. Eight men were Presidents from this state. Pick the one that interests you most. Make a time line of his life. With a friend make up a little skit that could have happened in his lifetime. Perform it for your class.

6. Jamestown was the first permanent American settlement. Research its history. Pretend you are a reporter interviewing one of the colonists. Find out how, when, where, why, and by whom it was colonized.

7. McCormick invented the reaper near Grove, Virginia. How has mechanization of farms helped our economy? Find an old picture of the reaper and compare it with the new ones.

8. A famous sea battle occurred off the coast of Virginia. It involved the *Monitor* and the *Merrimack*. One was wooden, the other iron. Find out which one won and why. Make your own little fleet. Use a bottle cap with a small bit of clay. Add a toothpick and a paper sail. This little boat is metal. Then using a very thin piece of wood, or cardboard, shape it like an iron. In the middle of the back, force a sliver of soap. Let it set for a few minutes, and it will start to move in the water.

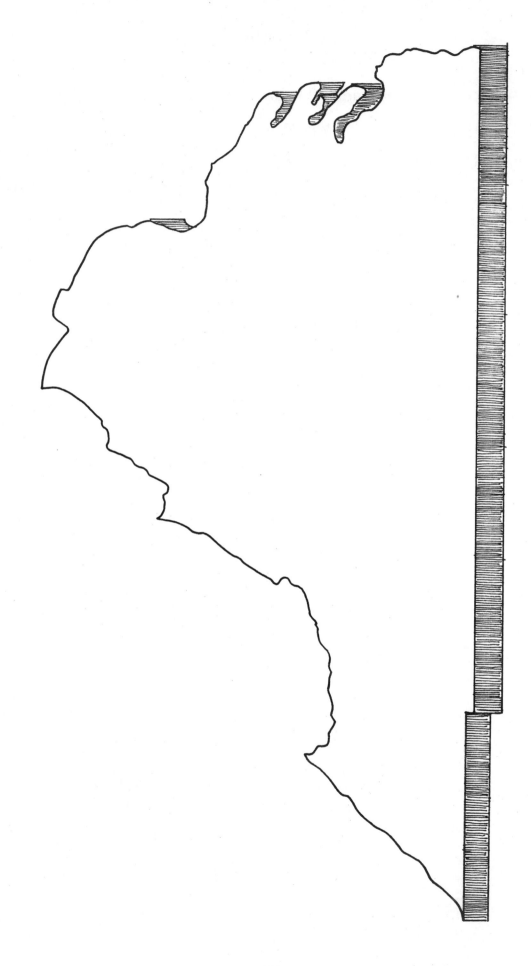

VIRGINIA

WASHINGTON

```
E
  Y R E B W A R T S W I L L O W R
  Q W A I N W R I G H T C P E A H
C G T L A S   V T U B I L A H U B E H O S G O O
              A S A B I R C H I E F I T T U K T D
O C L A R K Y   R N A G E K N A E S A I P O
A L L E W I K N A S S O T R I N S U U D
S D G U O R C R D L E U O O N E O P Y A G E
T F R N O E F U N C K L C L G O A M R E N
  I A E L B O M A E C J E T A K L I A Y T D
N V M M R I G K A O N T N A L K N E E L R
C E U T N A S S O A B N U A I F E E B O
H L H U A N K E M E K E P Y T A C O M A N
  M M S O P L S S N E R E V U O C N A V
  P O H A B U L B T N I M R E P P E P
  N I S Q U A L L Y
```

Cities
Spokane
Birch (Bay)
Olympia
Seattle
Tacoma
Usk
Kiona
Yakima
Otis (Orchards)

Rivers
Columbia
Snake
Okanogan
Lewis
Quinault
Nisqually

Minerals
Aluminum
Gravel
Granite
Manganese
Basalt
Clay

Products
Salmon
Strawberry
Sugar Beet (2)
Rye
Sole
Halibut
Beef
Lumber
Peppermint
Potato
Hop
Bulb
Bees
Fur

Indians
Puyallup
Chinook
Nooksack

Famous People
Wainwright
Puget
Clark
Chief Joseph (2)
Handforth
Cook
Vancouver

State Symbols
Bird: Willow Goldfinch (2)
Flower: Coast Rhododendron (2)
Tree: Western Hemlock (2)

Put the leftover letters all in a row. When you are through, the state nickname will show.

The _____ State

139

47

WASHINGTON

OBJECTIVES: To improve geographical knowledge of Washington.

To promote research skills.

To encourage knowledge of Washington's natural phenomena.

MATERIALS: An encyclopedia, paper bag, watercolors, yarn, salt, flour, and a small amount of water.

PROCEDURE: 1.   Do the word search and find the nickname.

2.   On the following page is a blank map of the state. Locate the listed cities and rivers. Draw them in on the state. Add five more cities and three more rivers of your own choosing.

3.   Make a legend for the minerals and products listed. Put these in. Color in the mountain ranges. Put in the areas where the Indian tribes roamed. Color code these.

4.   One tribe of Indians carved masks and things from wood. Make a mask from the paper bag like you think they might have used. Use the yarn for hair. Paint in bright colors on the bag. Find out which tribe or tribes used them. Make a picture that would have been typical of one of the tribal scenes.

5.   Mount Saint Helens has erupted only smoke and ash. Make a short report of this. How did it affect the surrounding country? Was it important? Why, or why not?

6.   In the Columbian Plateau are found ''Scablands'' and ''Coulees.'' What are these? Are they found anywhere else? How were they formed? How has modern control of rivers affected them? Using salt and flour, make a model of each on a piece of cardboard. Paint them as you think they look when they dry. Use twice as much flour as salt.

7.   Many tourists come to Washington to enjoy the recreation and scenery. Make a brochure advertising some of the facilities available in Washington.

WASHINGTON

WEST VIRGINIA

Cities
Charleston
Leon
Clarksburg
Huntington
Parkersburg

Rivers
Potomac
Shenandoah
Ohio
Monongahela
Gauley
New
Cheat
Kanawha

Indians
Conoy
Shawnee
Susquehanna

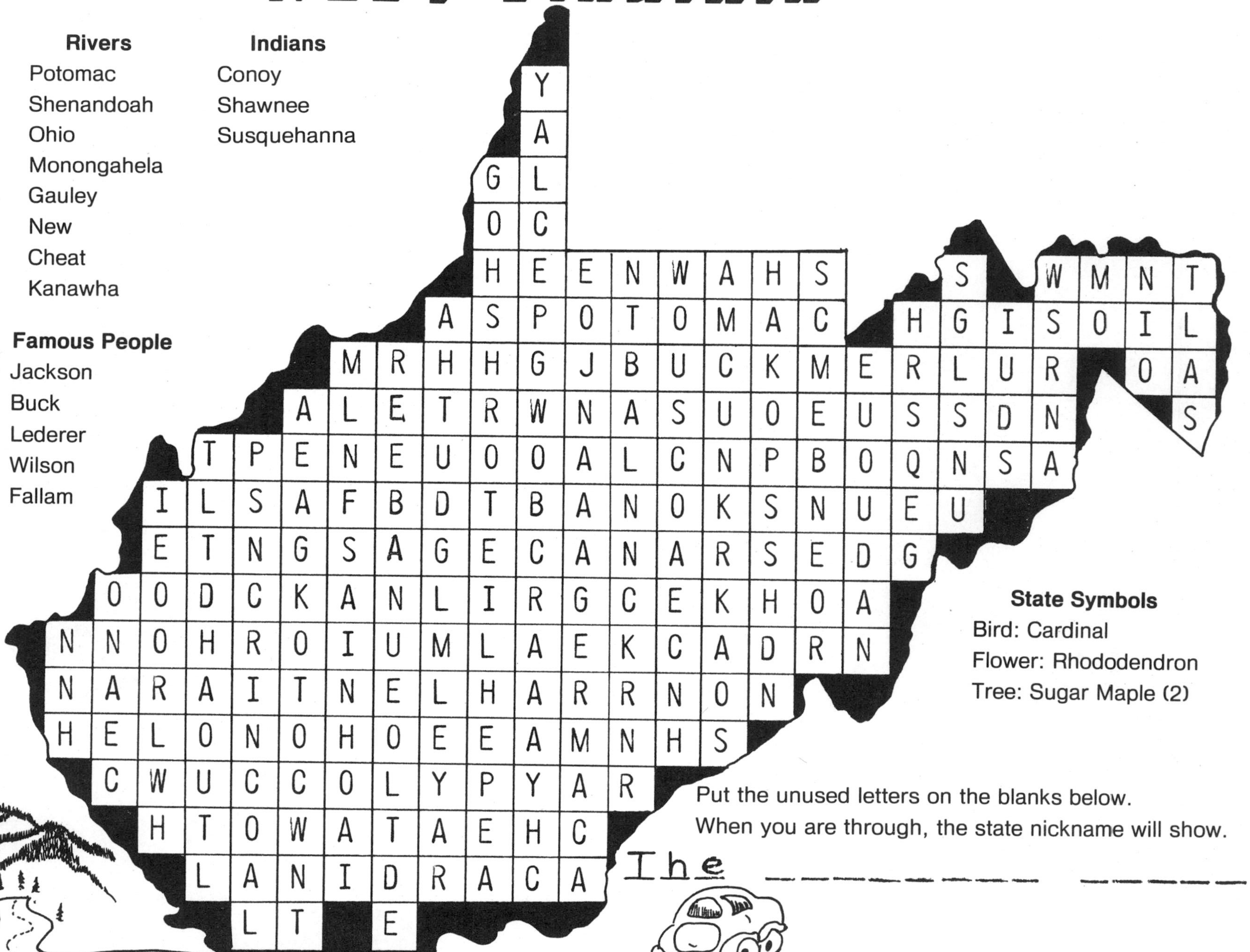

Products
Corn
Tobacco
Sheep
Wool
Hog
Chemical

Famous People
Jackson
Buck
Lederer
Wilson
Fallam

Minerals
Clay
Coal
Salt
Oil

State Symbols
Bird: Cardinal
Flower: Rhododendron
Tree: Sugar Maple (2)

Put the unused letters on the blanks below.
When you are through, the state nickname will show.

The _ _ _ _ _ _ _ _ _ _ _ _

48

WEST VIRGINIA

OBJECTIVES: To promote geographical knowledge of West Virginia.

To improve research skills.

To strengthen the cultural knowledge of West Virginia.

MATERIALS: An encyclopedia, cardboard, and a paper brad for a spinner.

PROCEDURE:
1. Do the word search and find the nickname.

2. On the following page is a blank map of West Virginia. Locate the cities and rivers listed on the word search. Draw in the rivers and put the cities in where they are located. Add five more cities and three more rivers of your choice.

3. Make a legend for the minerals and products of West Virginia. Put these on the map. Color in the mountain ranges. Add their names.

4. Travel is not easy in West Virginia, because it is a mountainous region. Some of the people who live back in the mountains rarely travel to the cities or very far from their homes. Make a gameboard for you and a friend to play using some of the obstacles you might encounter when traveling through the mountains. Pretend you are on horseback. Include such things as your horse strayed away, go back two spaces; you're traveling downhill, take an extra turn; your way is blocked by a rock slide, skip a turn; you find an old wagon trail, go ahead three spaces; a sudden blizzard makes you wait, skip two turns; you shoot a bear, go ahead two spaces; you get lost, go back three spaces; a friendly native tells you about a shortcut, take an extra turn; you meet another traveler on a narrow ledge, you must go back to let him pass and lose a turn; finish; you are in town. Use a spinner made of a circle with a paper brad for the center. Divide your circle into four spaces.

5. Make a list of the things you would have to do without if you had no electricity or running water. Pretend you live in the remote area of West Virginia. Make a list of the things you would have to do in the course of a day. Remember, there are no modern conveniences!

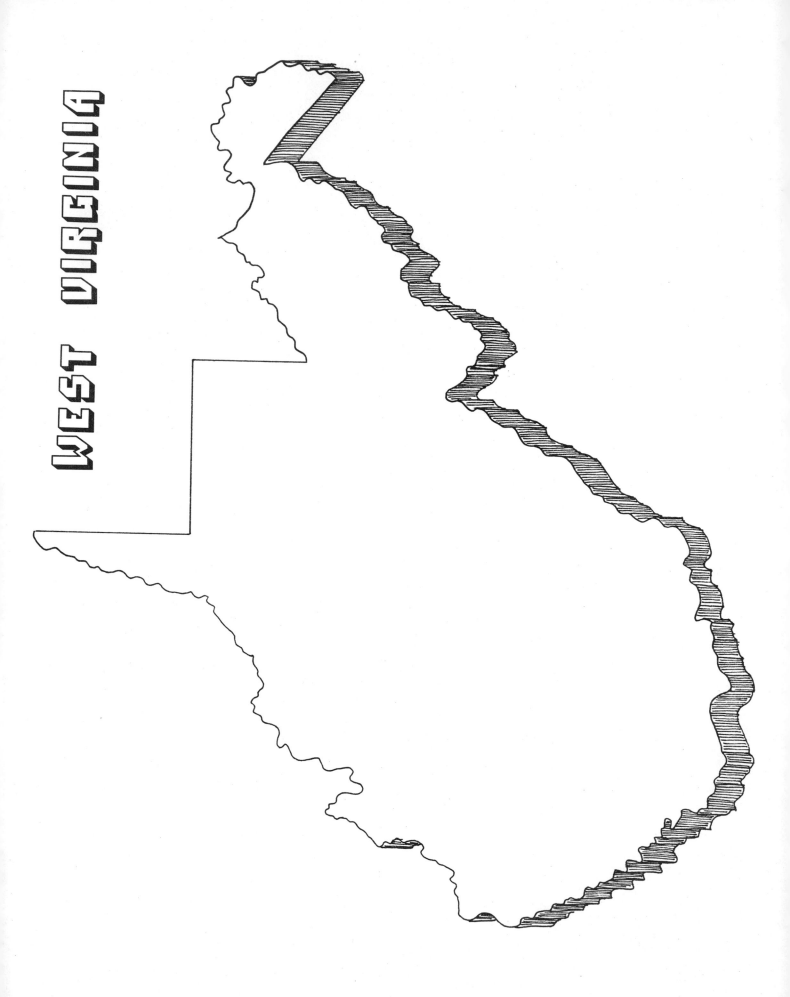

WEST VIRGINIA

WISCONSIN

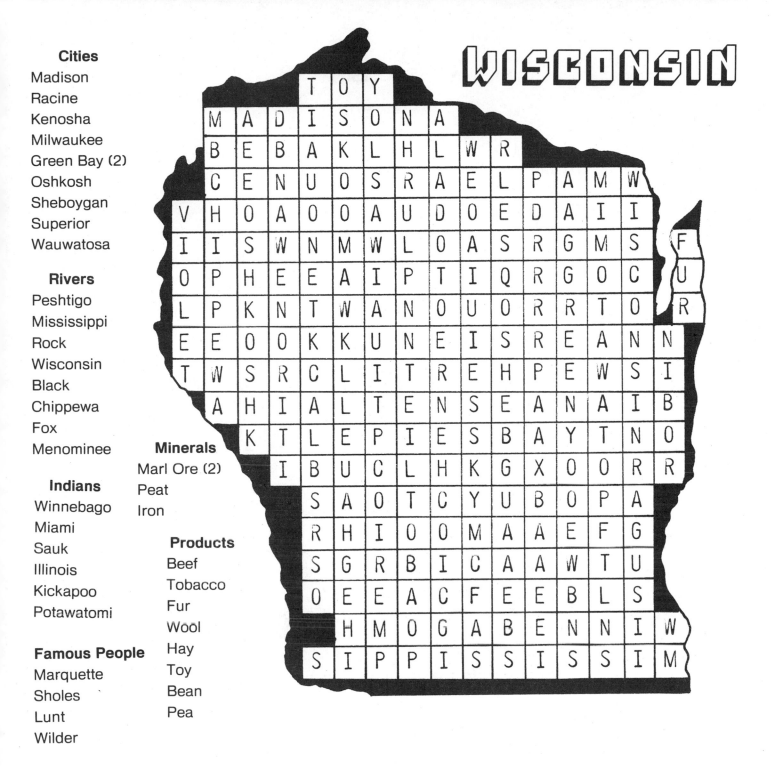

Cities
Madison
Racine
Kenosha
Milwaukee
Green Bay (2)
Oshkosh
Sheboygan
Superior
Wauwatosa

Rivers
Peshtigo
Mississippi
Rock
Wisconsin
Black
Chippewa
Fox
Menominee

Indians
Winnebago
Miami
Sauk
Illinois
Kickapoo
Potawatomi

Famous People
Marquette
Sholes
Lunt
Wilder

Minerals
Marl Ore (2)
Peat
Iron

Products
Beef
Tobacco
Fur
Wool
Hay
Toy
Bean
Pea

State Symbols
Bird: Robin
Flower: (Wood) Violet
Tree: Sugar Maple (2)

Please put leftover letters on the blanks below.
If you're correct, the nickname will show.

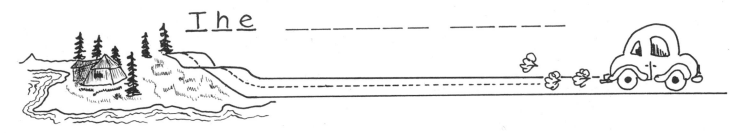

The _ _ _ _ _ _ _ _ _ _ _

145

49

WISCONSIN

OBJECTIVES: To promote geographical knowledge of Wisconsin.

To encourage research skills.

To enrich knowledge of social progress in Wisconsin.

MATERIALS: An encyclopedia, cardboard, and large map of the United States.

PROCEDURE: 1. Do the word search and find the state nickname.

2. On the following page is a blank map of the state. Put the cities and rivers listed in the word search. Draw in the rivers. Add three lakes and two rivers of your own choice. Add six more cities of your own choosing.

3. Make a legend for the minerals and products listed. Put these in on your map. Color code the areas the Indians live in.

4. On a large cardboard, in sequence, put in the social reforms first started in Wisconsin. Include Mothers' Pensions, Workers' Compensation, Minimum Wage Laws, Old-Age Pensions, Teachers' Pensions, and Unemployment Compensation.

5. Research one of the famous people listed. Write a short biography to share with your class.

6. On a large United States map, trace the path of the first explorers of Wisconsin: Marquette and Joliet, Nicolet, Allouez, and Andre.

7. In a short essay, explain why Wisconsin is known as ''America's Dairyland.'' Be sure to include the Swiss immigrants as well as the cheese makers from New York.

WISCONSIN

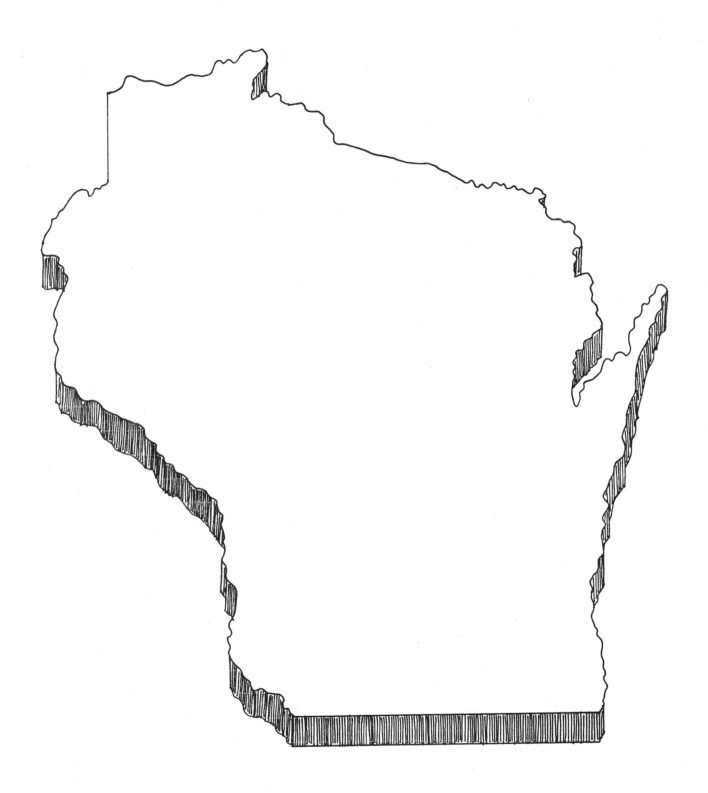

WYOMING

Y	B	L	A	C	K	F	O	O	T	E	T	I	N	O	T	N	E	B	I
E	R	O	O	B	T	E	H	D	E	B	R	I	D	G	E	R	U	S	N
L	E	O	N	O	A	E	I	K	A	U	Q	N	S	U	L	F	U	R	D
L	T	L	S	N	W	N	C	K	O	R	R	U	O	L	F	G	F	U	I
O	L	L	I	S	E	O	N	S	A	O	O	S	I	A	A	L	Y	N	A
W	O	E	A	R	L	V	S	O	C	H	A	L	L	R	A	D	R	I	N
S	C	W	B	L	O	I	N	C	L	S	O	O	T	O	O	B	N	D	
T	U	O	O	P	M	N	A	L	G	K	A	A	H	C	H	M	O	O	O
O	H	P	Y	L	M	D	I	U	L	B	L	E	W	G	U	J	H	H	O
N	A	P	E	A	I	A	O	O	S	E	A	L	I	L	T	A	A	S	W
E	Y	E	T	R	L	D	C	A	B	D	O	B	O	M	E	D	P	O	N
L	B	E	E	F	I	C	R	O	W	R	C	C	E	V	A	E	A	H	O
A	W	H	E	A	T	O	R	E	P	S	A	C	R	I	E	R	R	S	T
R	S	S	B	T	K	K	R	A	L	C	T	R	O	N	A	L	A	Y	T
K	W	O	D	A	E	M	P	H	O	S	P	H	A	T	E	G	L	L	O
G	O	H	S	U	R	B	T	N	I	A	P	E	N	N	E	Y	E	H	C

Cities
Cheyenne
Casper
Laramie
Sheridan
Douglas
Cody
Lovell
Superior
Buffalo
Powell
Clark

Rivers
Absaroka
Missouri
Colorado
Columbia
Yellowstone
Bighorn
Niobrara

Minerals
Sulfur Ore (2)
Bentonite
Phosphate
Jade
Trona
Coal
Iron Ore (2)
Clay
Oil
Gas

Famous People
Colter
Bonneville
Ross
Campbell
Bridger
Pollock
Washakie

Indians
Arapaho
Bannock
Blackfoot
Crow
Flathead
Shoshoni
Ute

Products

Sugar Beet (2)	Hay
Wool	Sheep
Bee	Wheat
Flour	Hog
Corn	Beef

State Symbols
Bird: Meadow Lark (2)
Flower: Indian Paintbrush (2)
Tree: Cottonwood

EXIT

Put the unused letters all in a row.
If you're right, the state nickname you'll know.

_ _ _ _ _ _ _ _ _ _
State

WYOMING

OBJECTIVES: To increase geographical knowledge about Wyoming.

To improve research skills.

To promote interest in Wyoming's natural phenomena.

MATERIALS: An encyclopedia and a large piece of cardboard.

PROCEDURE: 1.   Solve the word search and find the state's nickname.

2.   On the following page is a blank map of the state. Locate the cities and draw in the rivers listed. Add five more cities of your own choosing and three more rivers.

3.   Make a legend for the minerals and products listed on the word search. Add these to the state on the next page.

4.   The first national monument was established in Wyoming in 1906. Research this. Illustrate it along with its history for a report to your class.

5.   Yellowstone Park was declared the first national park in 1872. Compare a national monument with a national park. Geothermal heat is the source of Iceland's energy. Write an essay on whether or not such a source would be feasible for us to consider.

6.   Over two hundred active geysers are found in Yellowstone. What causes them? Make a brochure advertising the park. Be sure to include geysers, hot springs, sparkling lakes, high waterfalls, deep gorges, and beautiful canyons.

7.   Women were given the right to vote in 1869 in Wyoming. In 1870, Esther Morris was the first female justice of the peace. In 1925, Nellie Ross was the first female governor in our country. Pick one and with a friend plan a skit to portray an episode from her life.

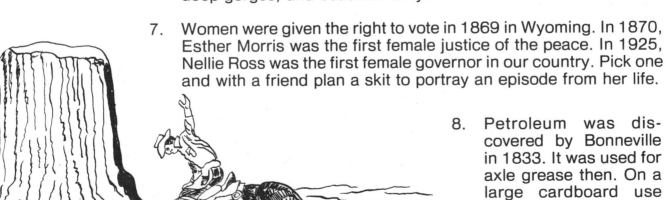

8.   Petroleum was discovered by Bonneville in 1833. It was used for axle grease then. On a large cardboard use about six illustrations to show its history from then until now.

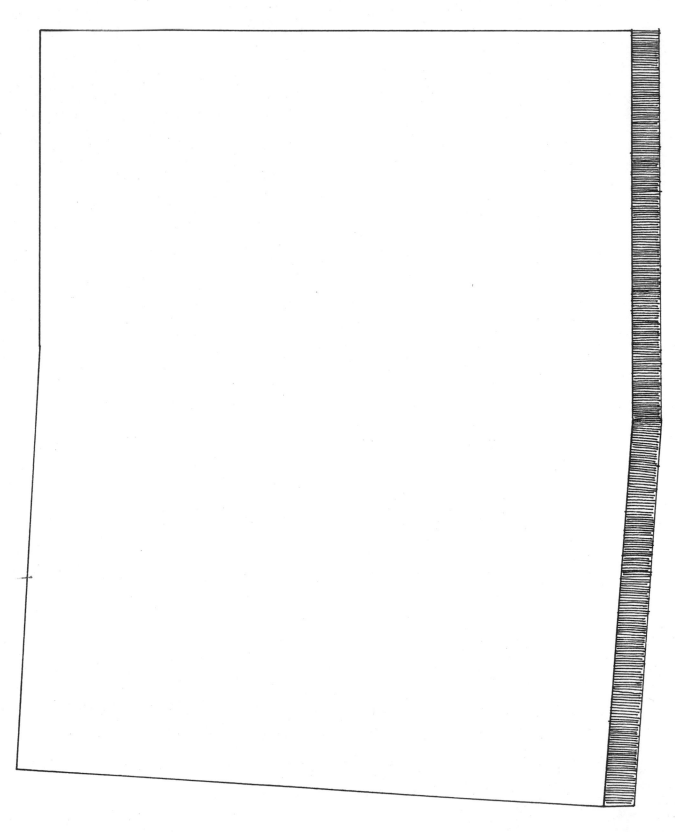

WYOMING

ANSWER KEY

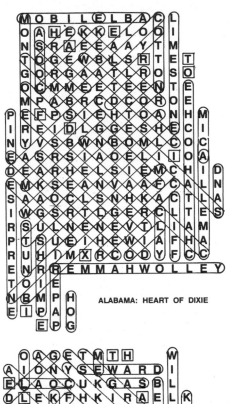

ALABAMA: HEART OF DIXIE

ALASKA: THE LAST FRONTIER

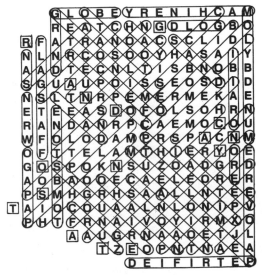

ARIZONA: GRAND CANYON STATE

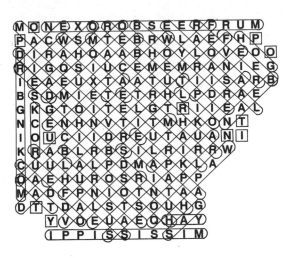

ARKANSAS: OPPORTUNITY

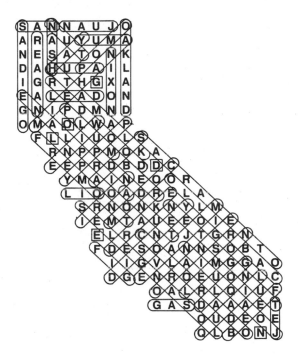

CALIFORNIA: GOLDEN

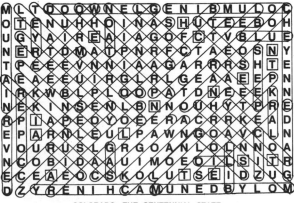

COLORADO: THE CENTENNIAL STATE

151

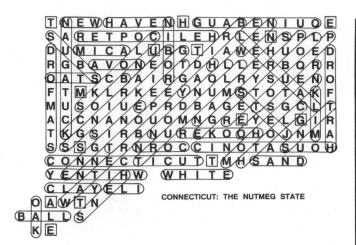

CONNECTICUT: THE NUTMEG STATE

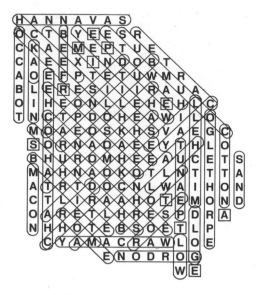

GEORGIA: EMPIRE STATE

DELAWARE: FIRST STATE

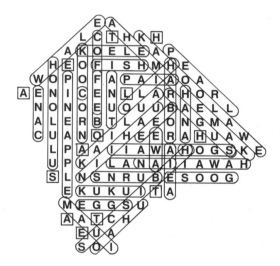

HAWAII: THE ALOHA STATE

FLORIDA: SUNSHINE

IDAHO: THE GEM STATE

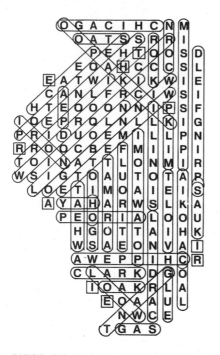

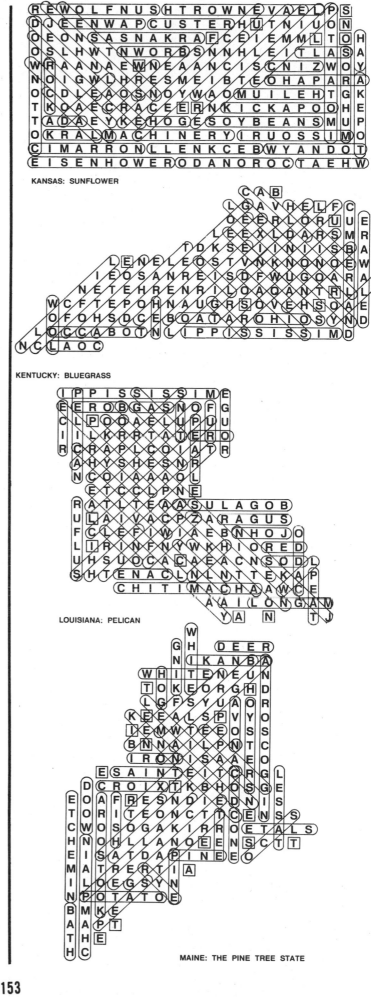

ILLINOIS: THE PRAIRIE

KANSAS: SUNFLOWER

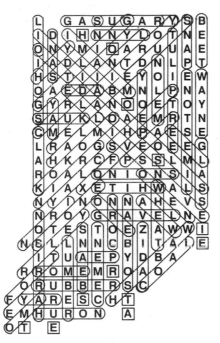

KENTUCKY: BLUEGRASS

INDIANA: HOOSIER STATE

LOUISIANA: PELICAN

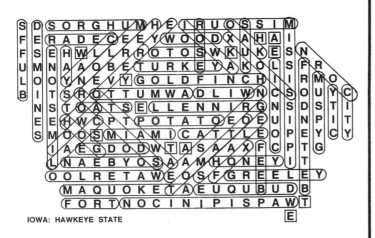

IOWA: HAWKEYE STATE

MAINE: THE PINE TREE STATE

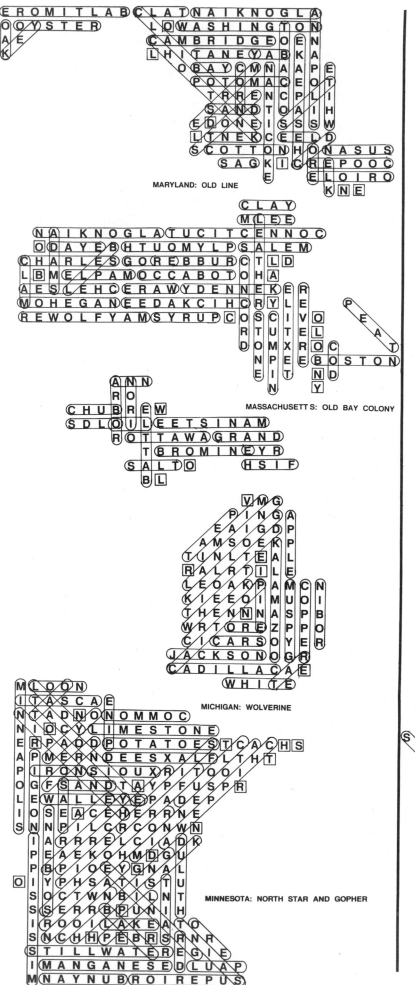
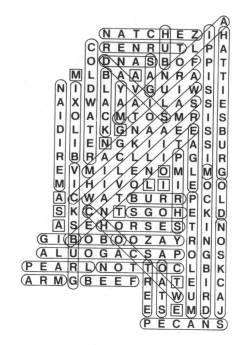
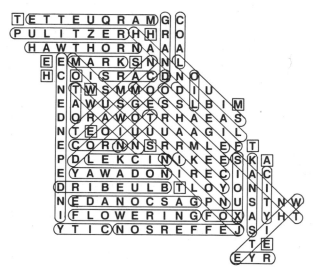
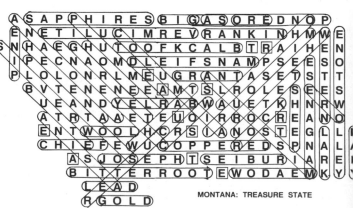

MARYLAND: OLD LINE

MASSACHUSETTS: OLD BAY COLONY

MICHIGAN: WOLVERINE

MINNESOTA: NORTH STAR AND GOPHER

MISSISSIPPI: MAGNOLIA STATE

MISSOURI: THE SHOW ME STATE

MONTANA: TREASURE STATE

154

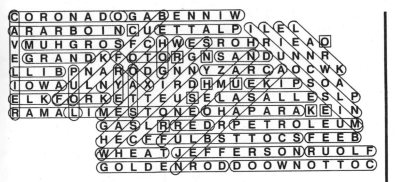

NEBRASKA: CORNHUSKER

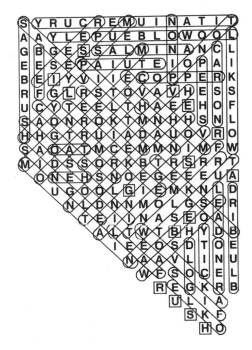

NEVADA: SILVER, SAGEBRUSH

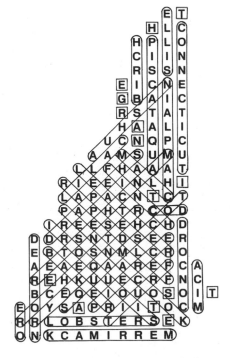

NEW HAMPSHIRE: THE GRANITE STATE

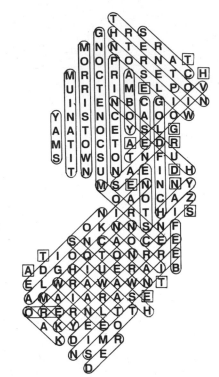

NEW JERSEY: THE GARDEN STATE

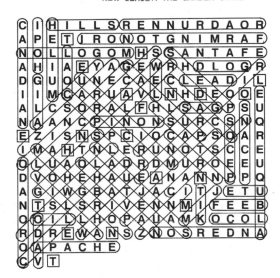

NEW MEXICO: THE LAND OF ENCHANTMENT

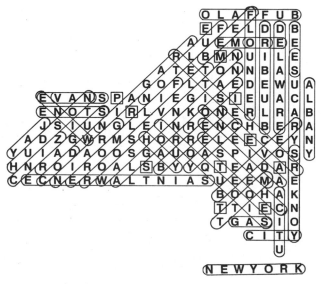

NEW YORK: EMPIRE STATE

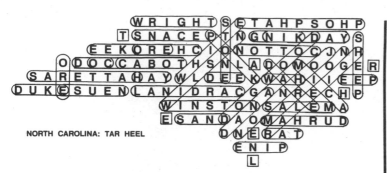

NORTH CAROLINA: TAR HEEL

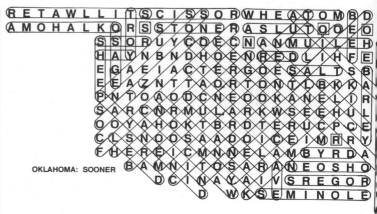

OKLAHOMA: SOONER

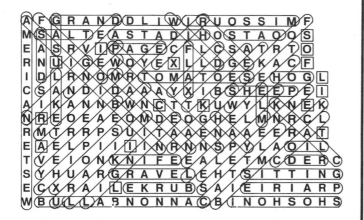

NORTH DAKOTA: SOUIX, FLICKERTAIL

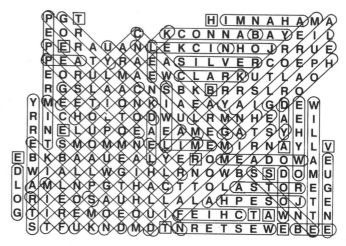

OREGON: THE BEAVER STATE

OHIO: THE BUCKEYE STATE

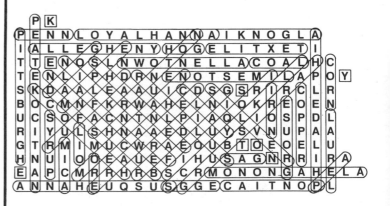

PENNSYLVANIA: KEYSTONE

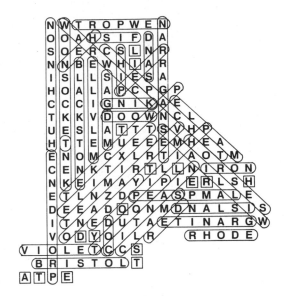

RHODE ISLAND: LITTLE RHODY STATE

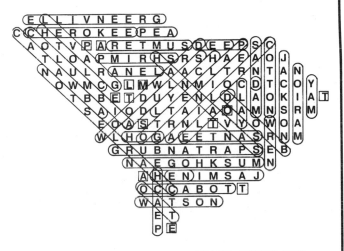

SOUTH CAROLINA: PALMETTO STATE

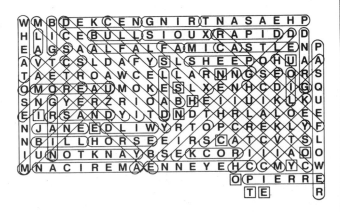

SOUTH DAKOTA: SUNSHINE, COYOTE

TENNESSEE: VOLUNTEER

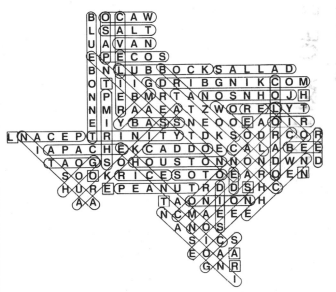

TEXAS: THE LONE STAR

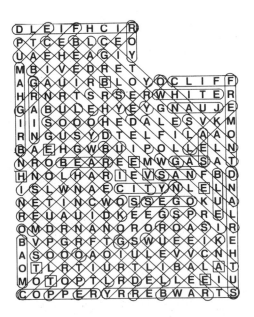

UTAH: BEEHIVE STATE

157

VERMONT: GREEN MOUNTAIN

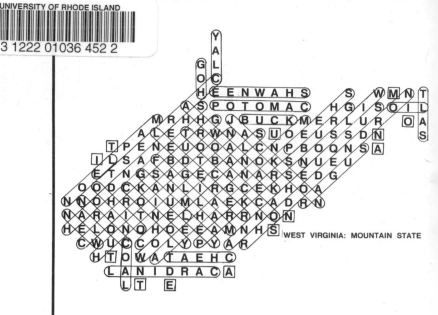

WEST VIRGINIA: MOUNTAIN STATE

VIRGINIA: OLD DOMINION

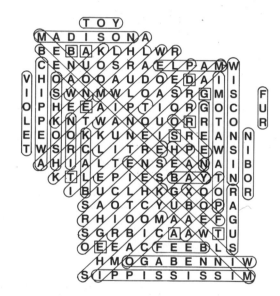

WISCONSIN: BADGER STATE

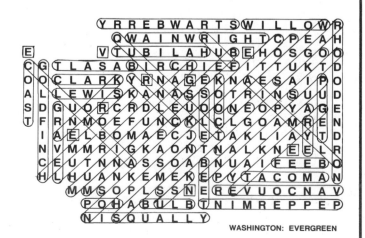

WASHINGTON: EVERGREEN

WYOMING: THE EQUALITY

158